I0491219

Sandru's Art Collection

Abstract Dreams

Coloring Book 1

Dumitru Sandru

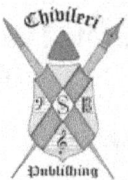

Chivileri Publishing

Copyright © 2016 by Dumitru Sandru

All artwork Copyright © 2016 by Dumitru Sandru

All rights reserved

ISBN 13: 978-1-942612-12-4

Disclaimer:

All rights reserved. No part of this book or the designs in this coloring book may be reproduced or transmitted in any form, or by any means, digital, electronic, Internet, or mechanical, including photocopying, scanning, digitizing, or recording for commercial purposes without permission in writing from Chivileri Publishing.

Exception allowed for inclusions in magazines or websites reviews, critiques, and other non-commercial uses permitted by copyright laws.

Acknowledgement:

The following designs are from Book 1 of Abstract and Surreal Drawings by Dumitru Sandru. Each drawing is identified by the number assigned in his catalog.

Dear friend,

Creative inspirations are good for your soul and once exercised they will bring you happiness, tranquility, and fulfillment in your life.

Although each design in this book may inspire a different picture in the mind of each viewer, after coloring it, or depending on what color combinations you may use the final drawing may be completely different from the one thought originally.

All you need to do is grab your coloring pencils or medium, relax, and give life to the drawings in this book.

Enjoy and have a good time.

For more information on the artist's works visit him at www.sandru.com

Dumitru Sandru,

Artist, Author and Composer

www.sandru.com

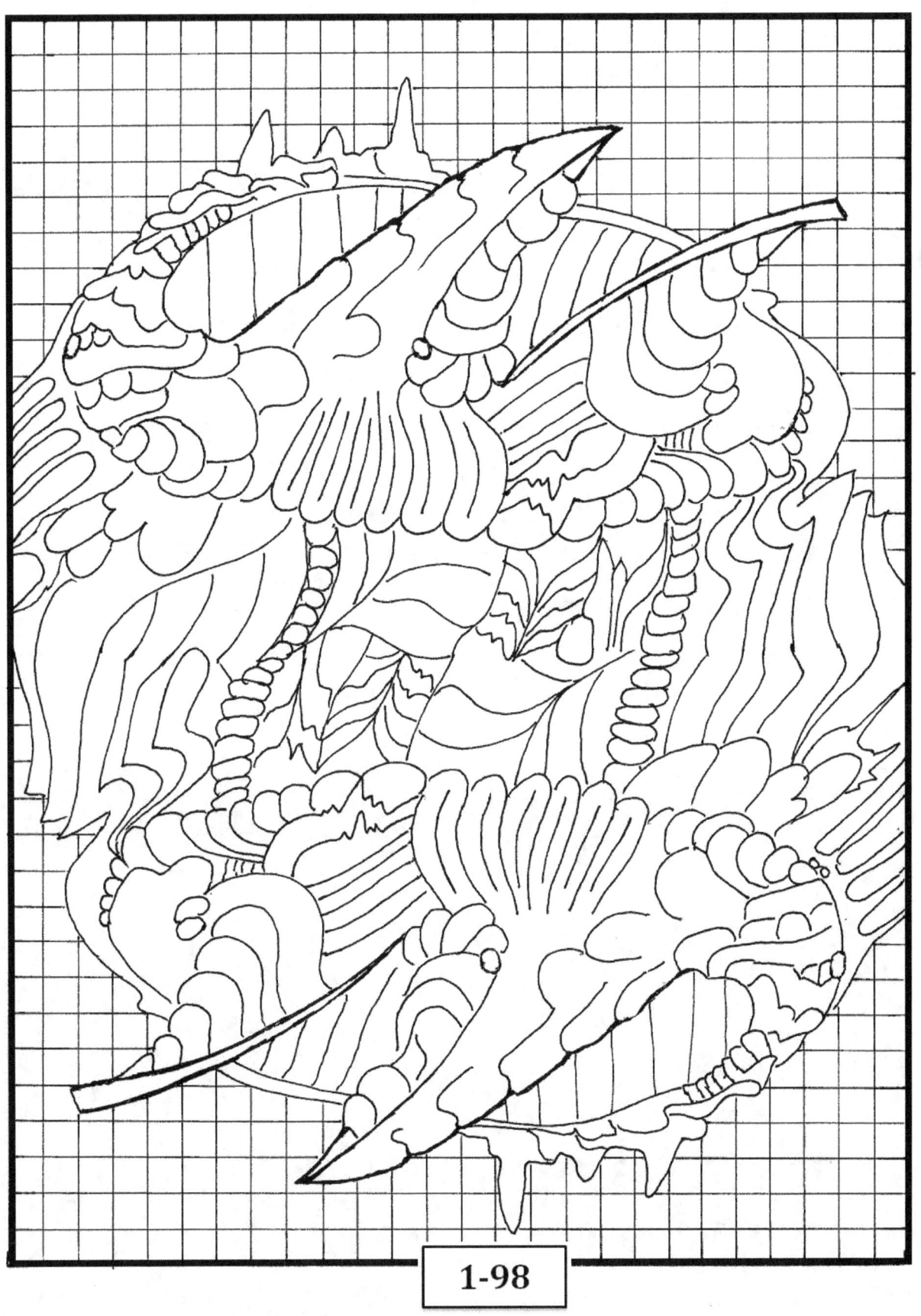

1-98

www.sandru.com

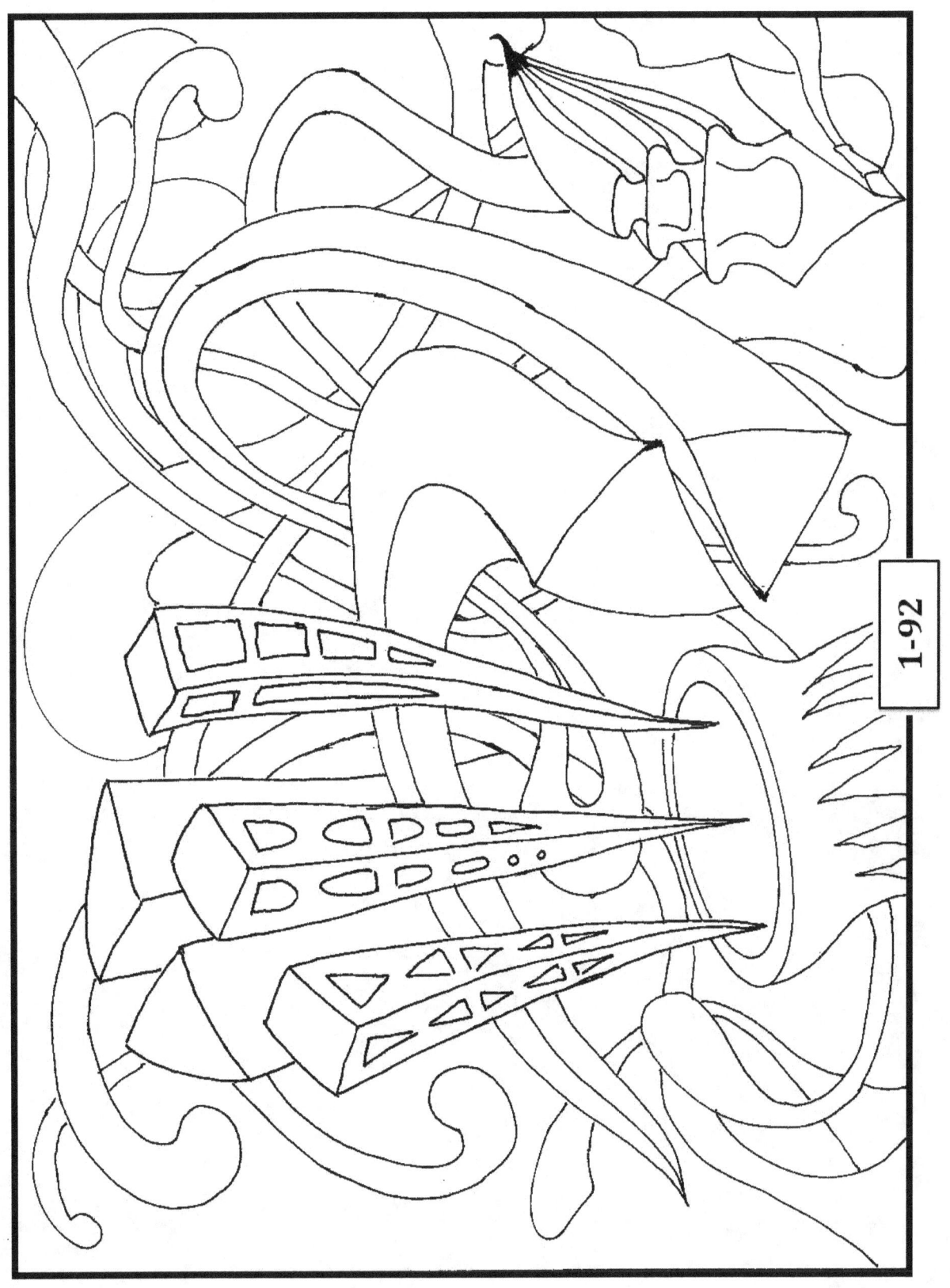

1-92

www.sandru.com

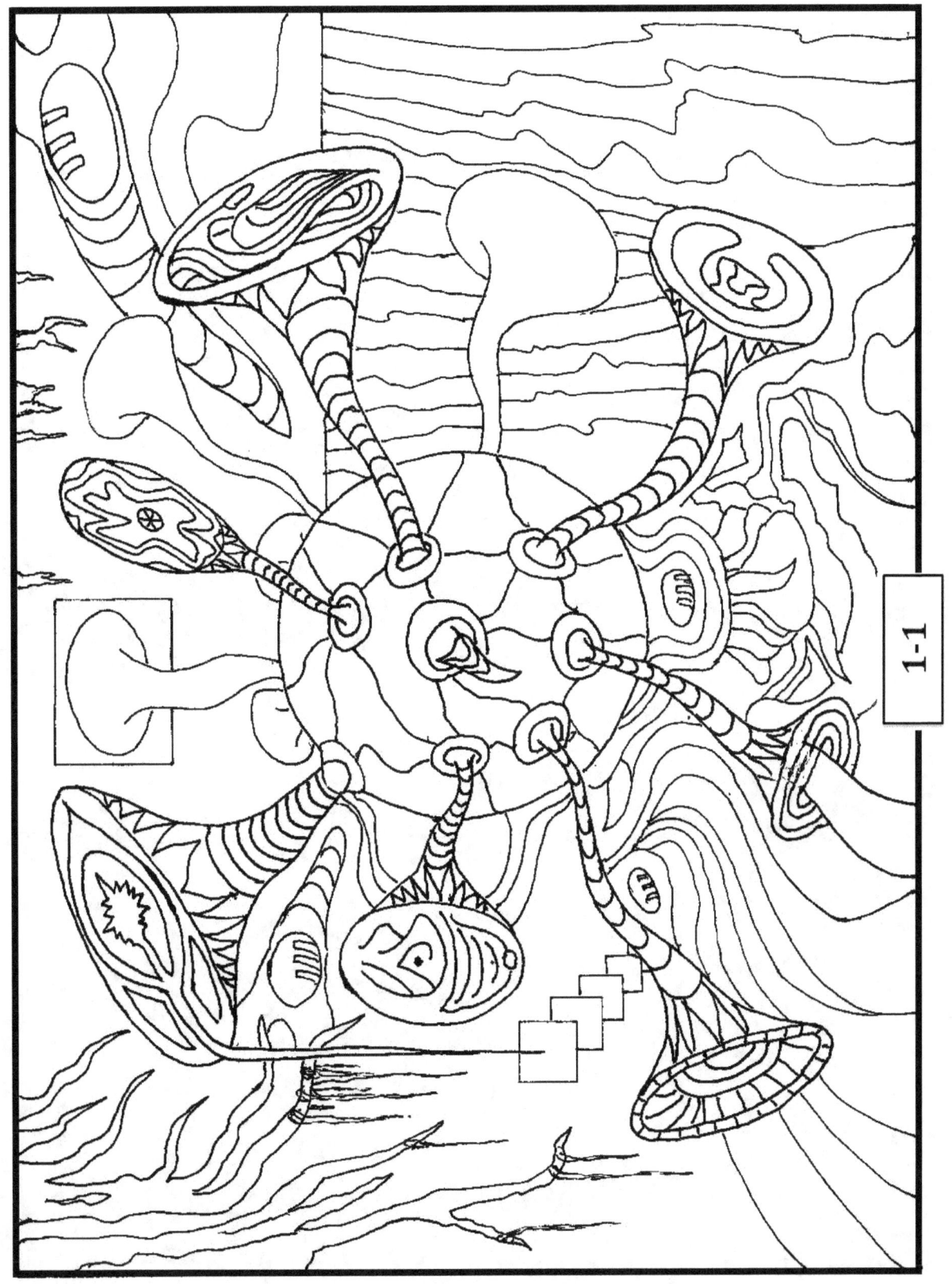

1-1

www.sandru.com

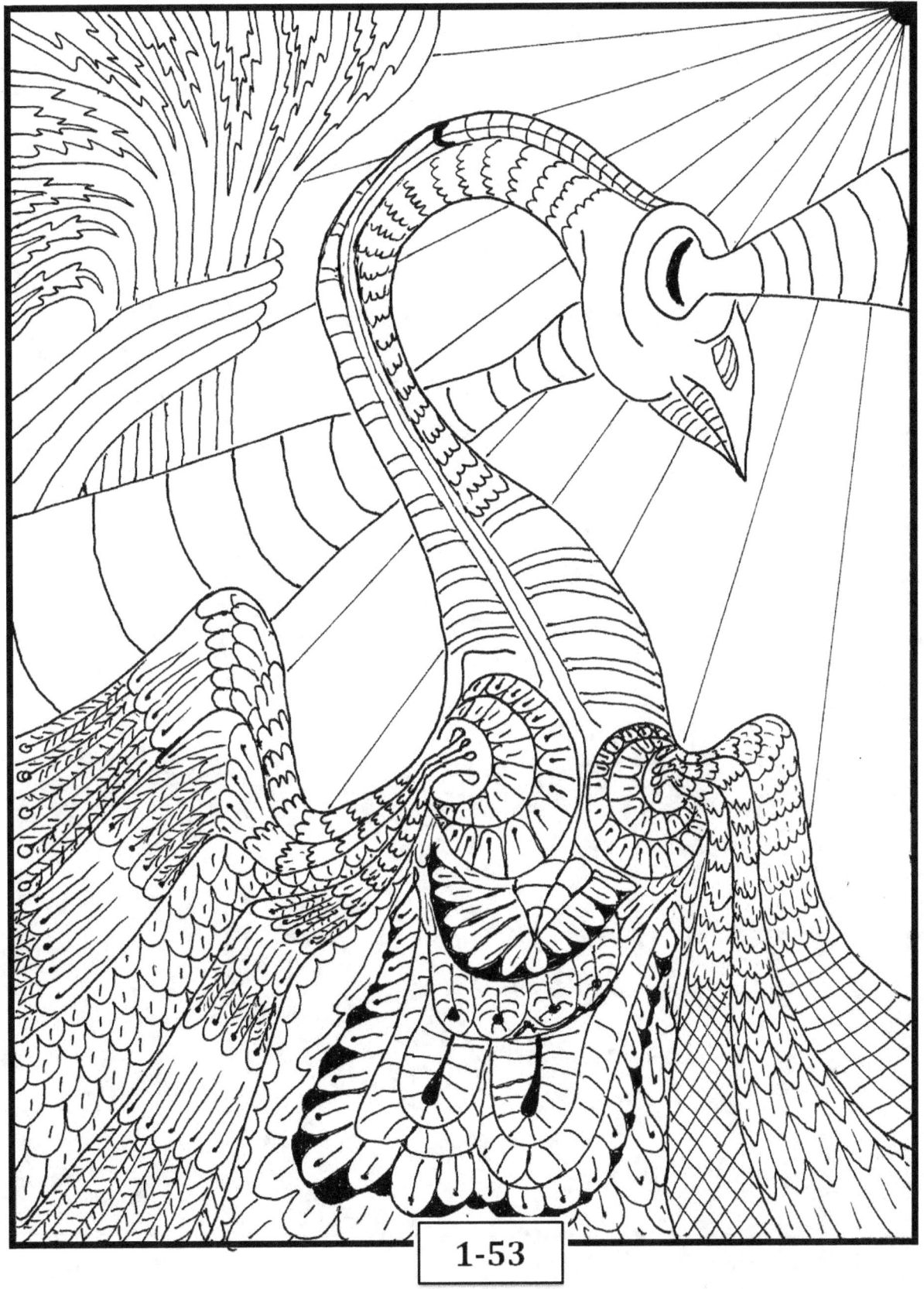

1-53

www.sandru.com

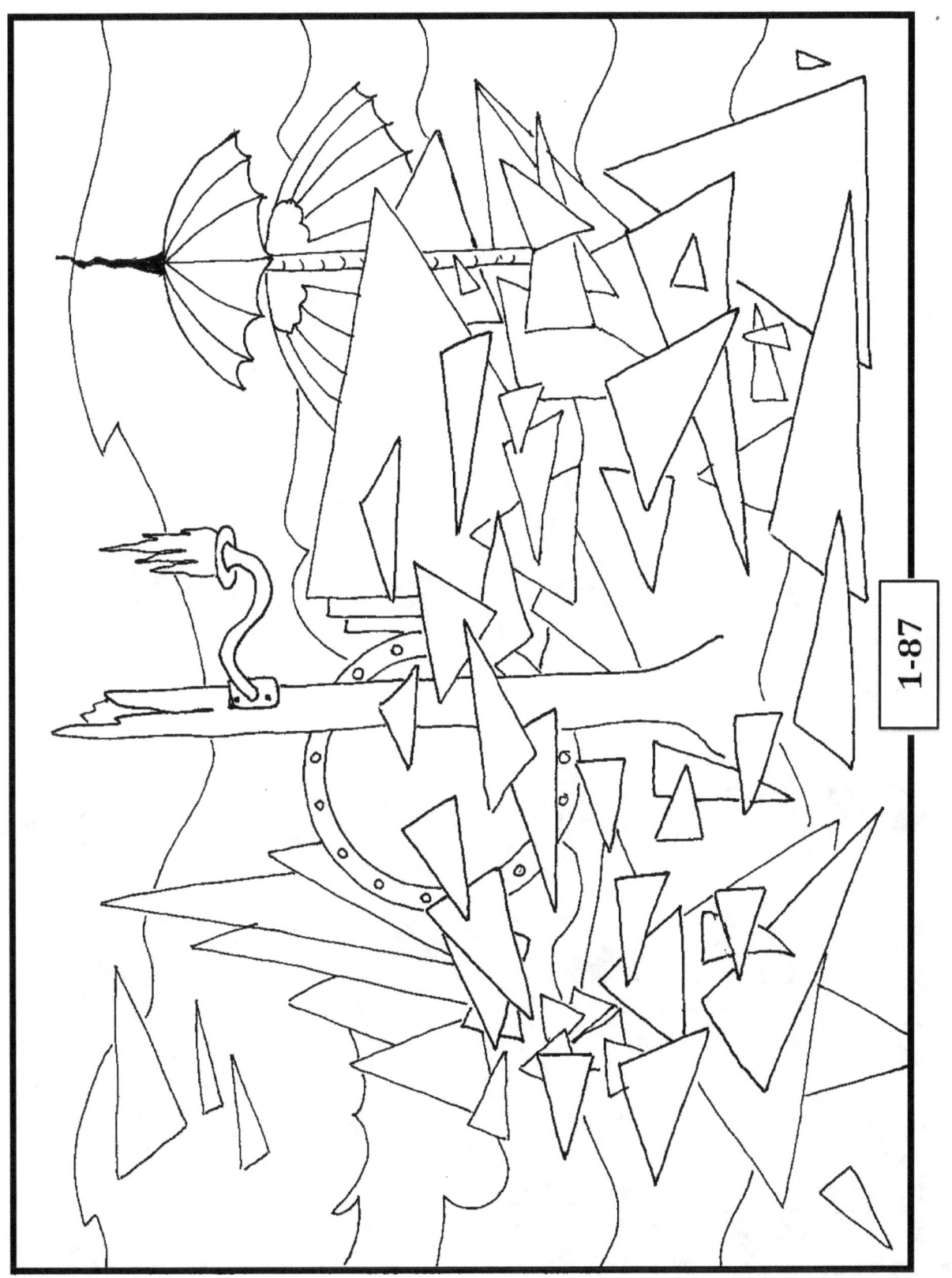

1-87

13

www.sandru.com

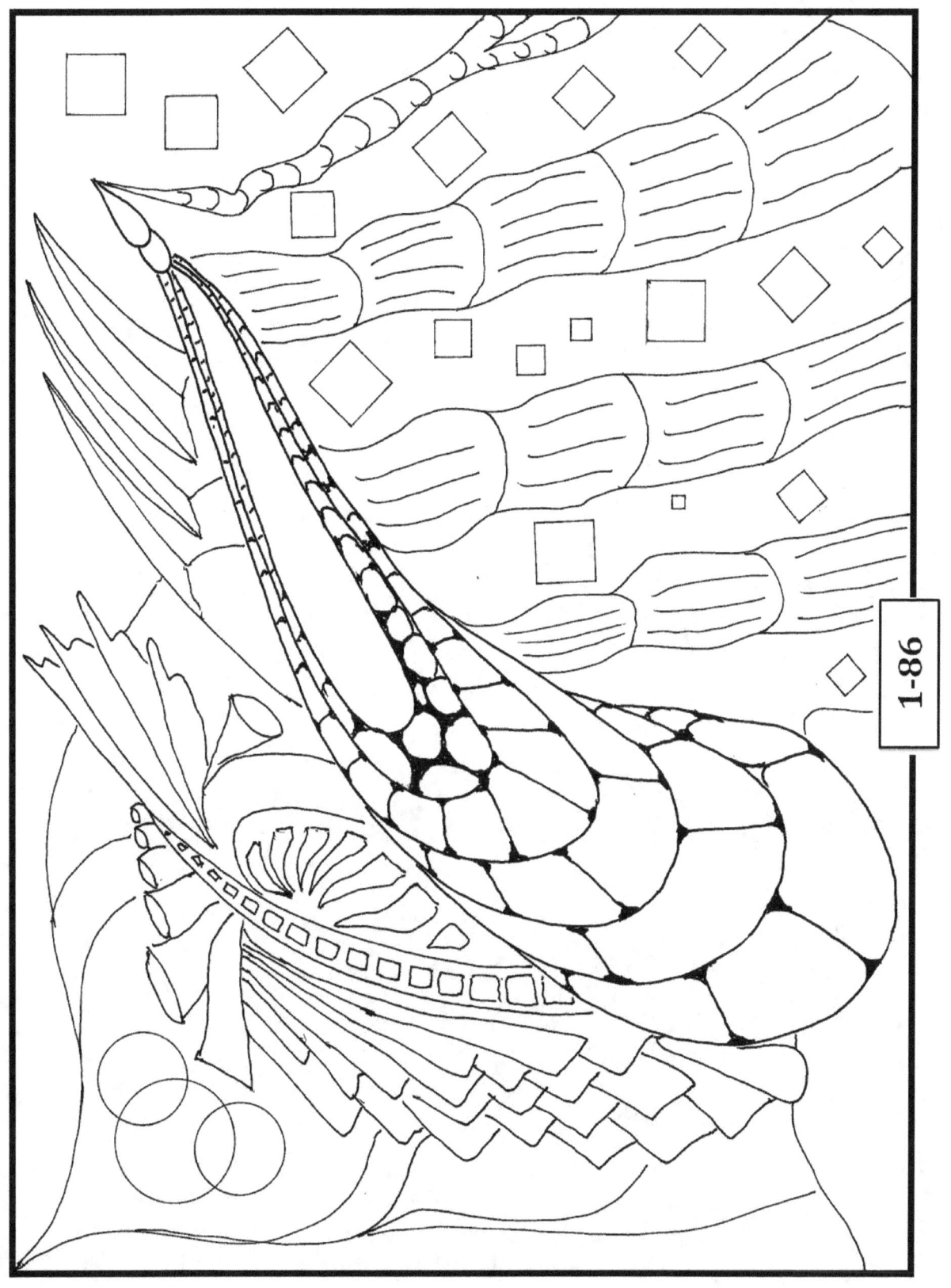

1-86

15

www.sandru.com

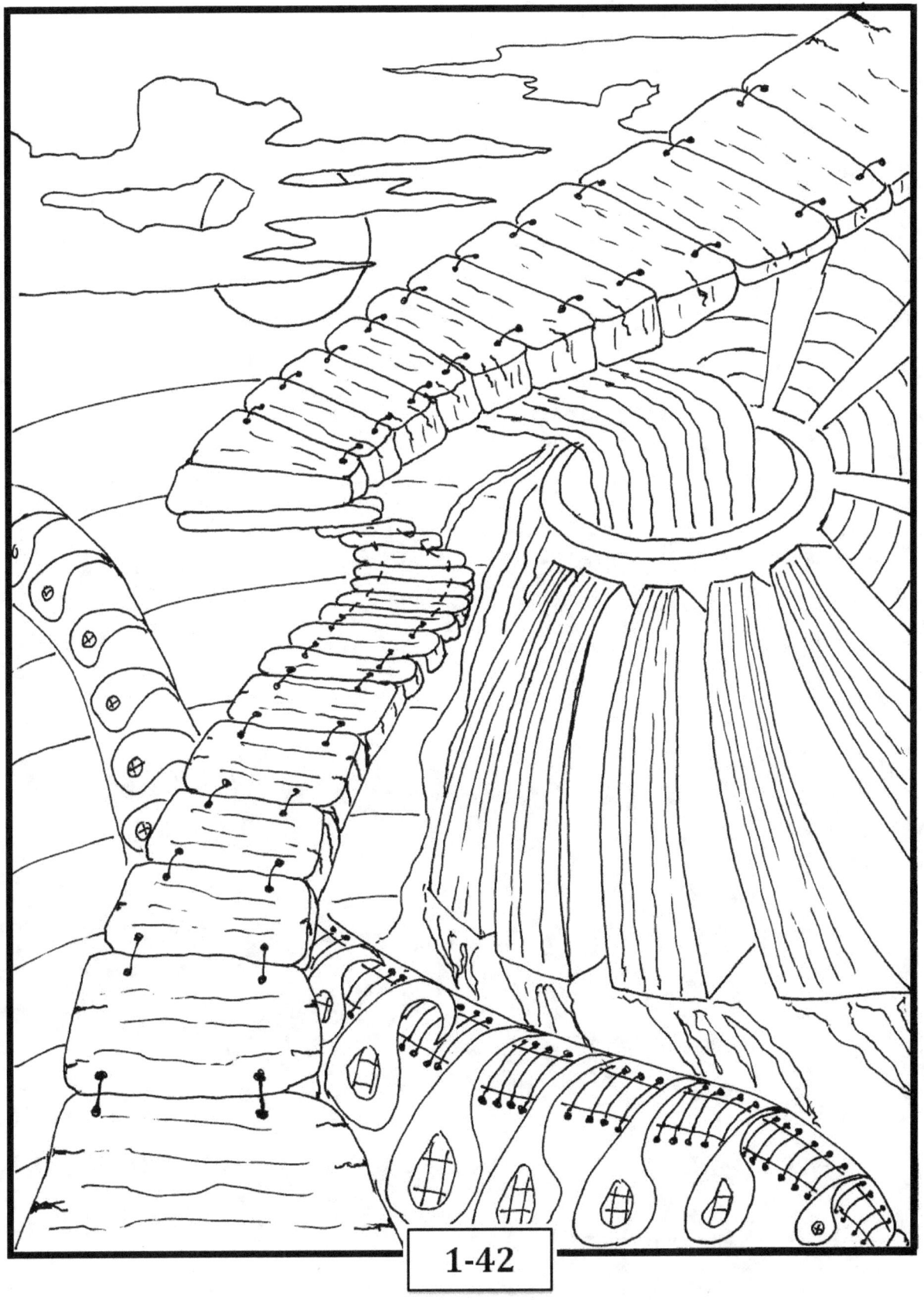

1-42

17

www.sandru.com

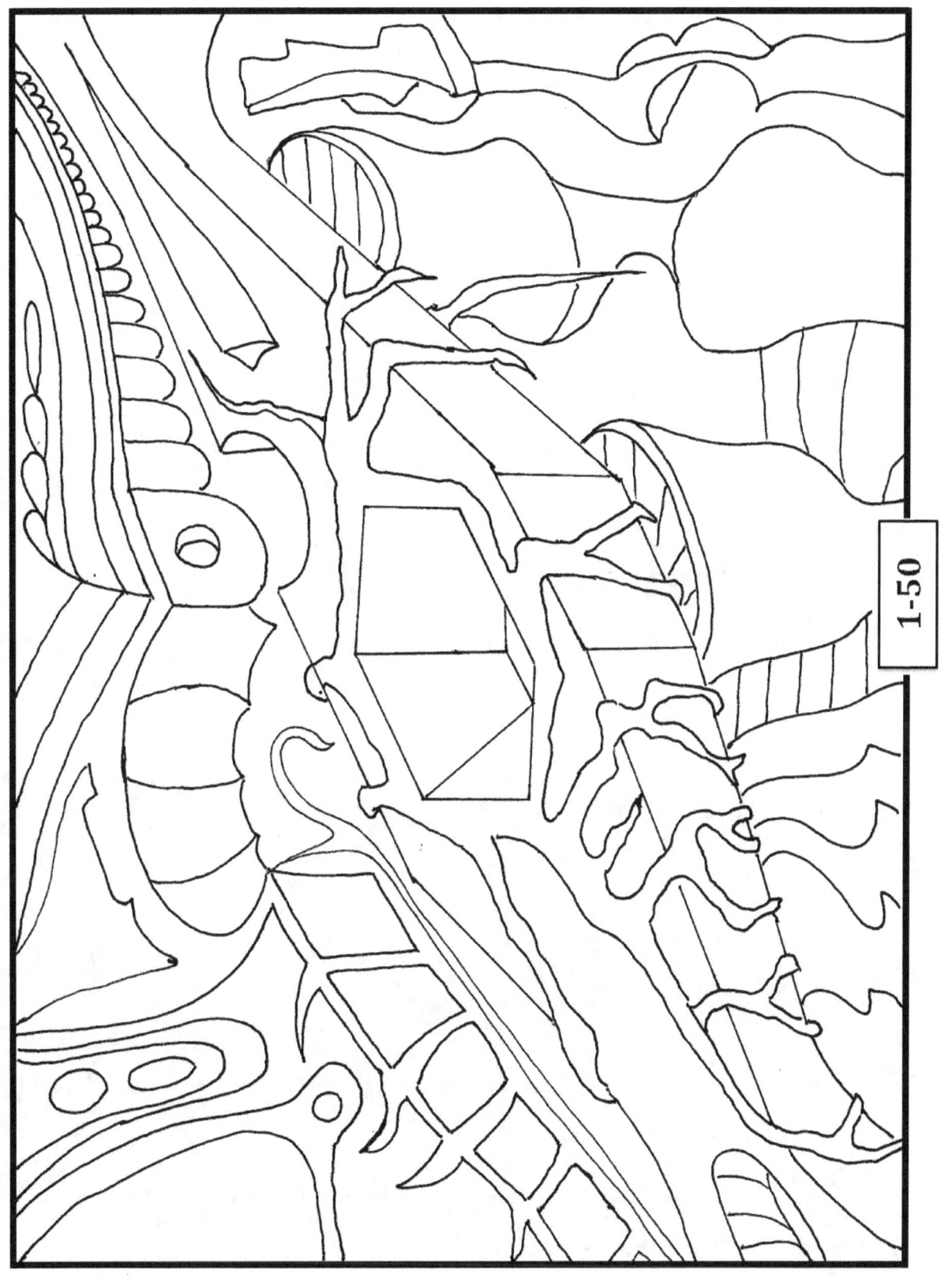

1-50

19

www.sandru.com

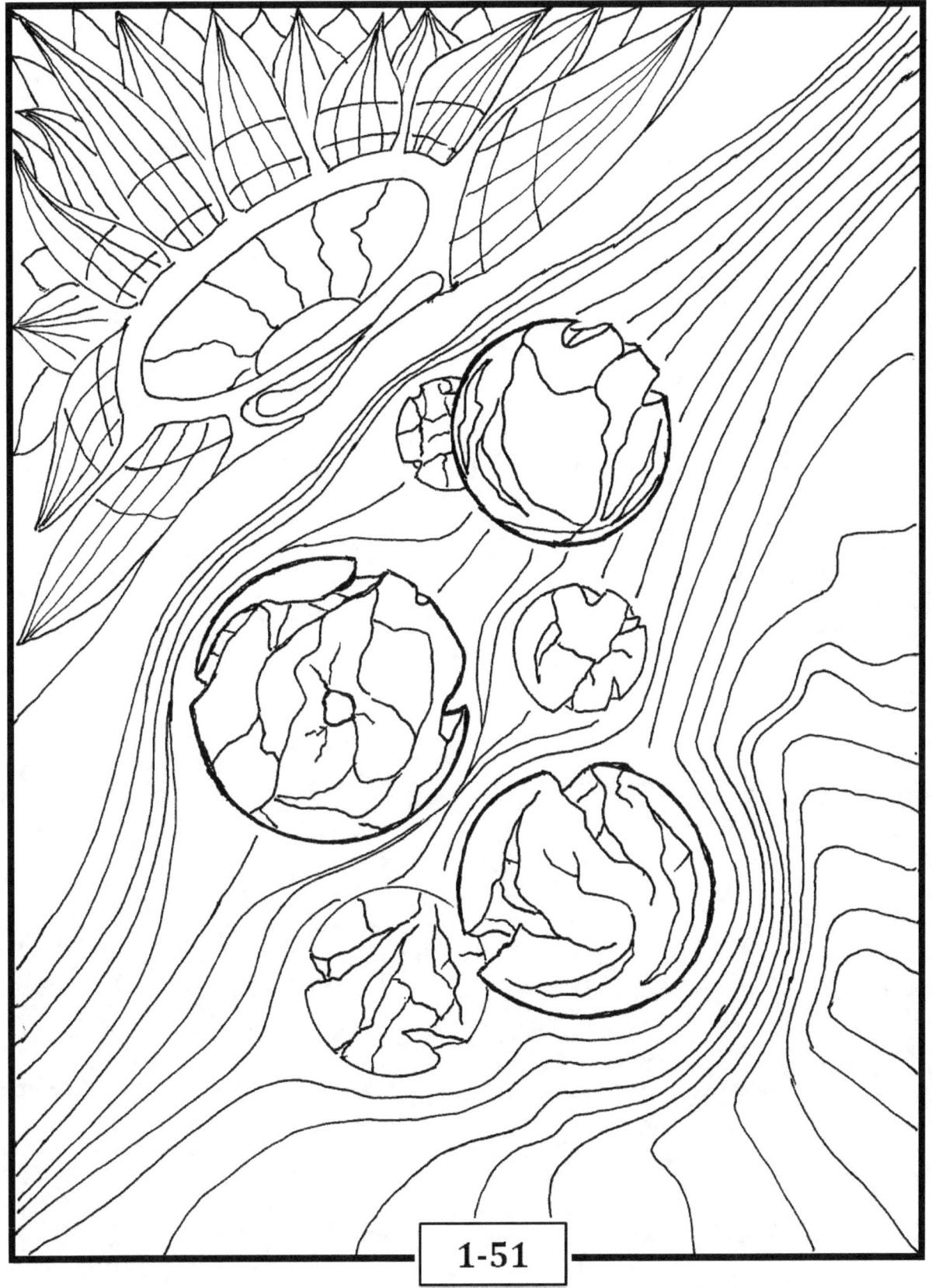

1-51

www.sandru.com

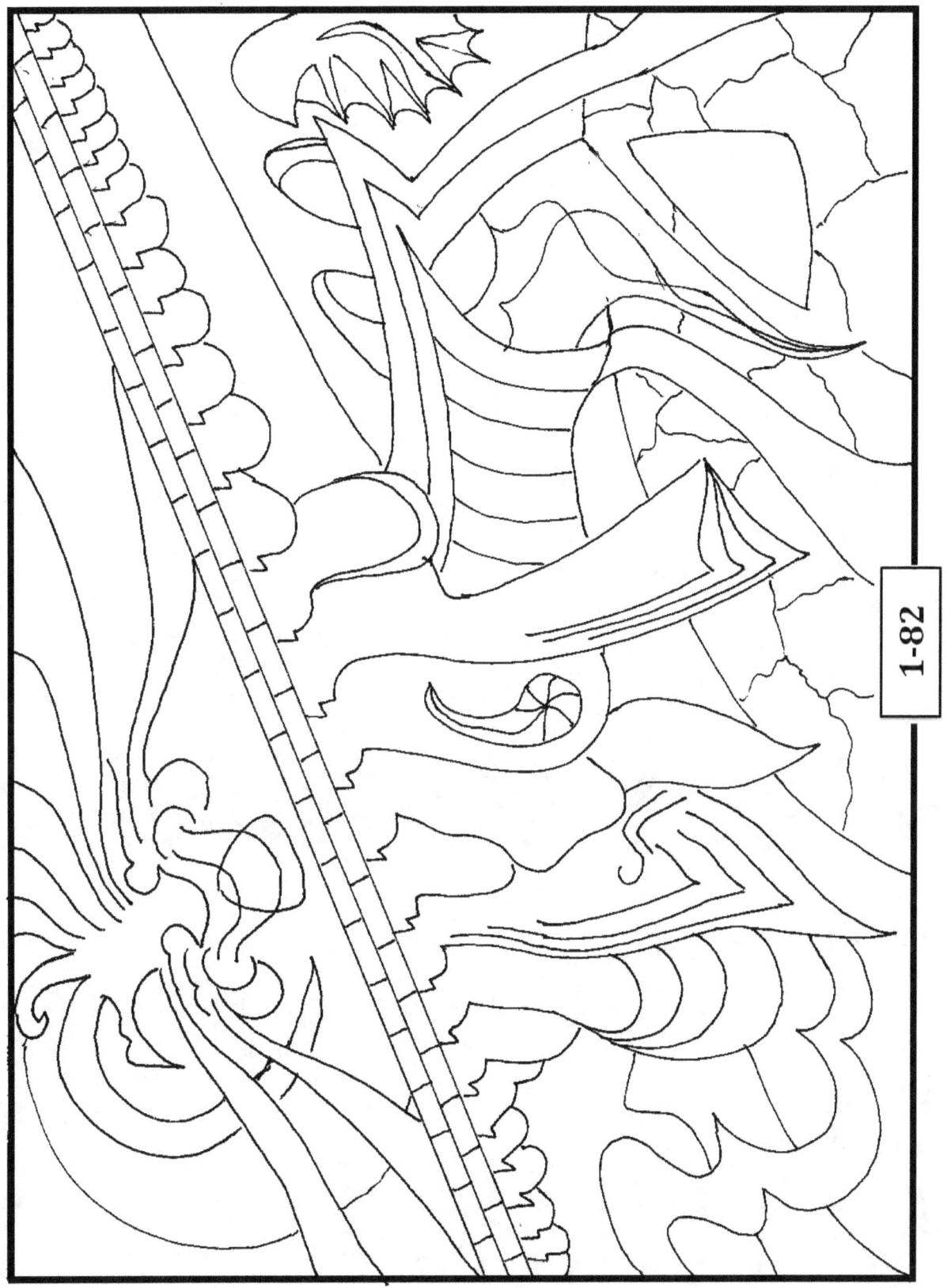

1-82

23

www.sandru.com

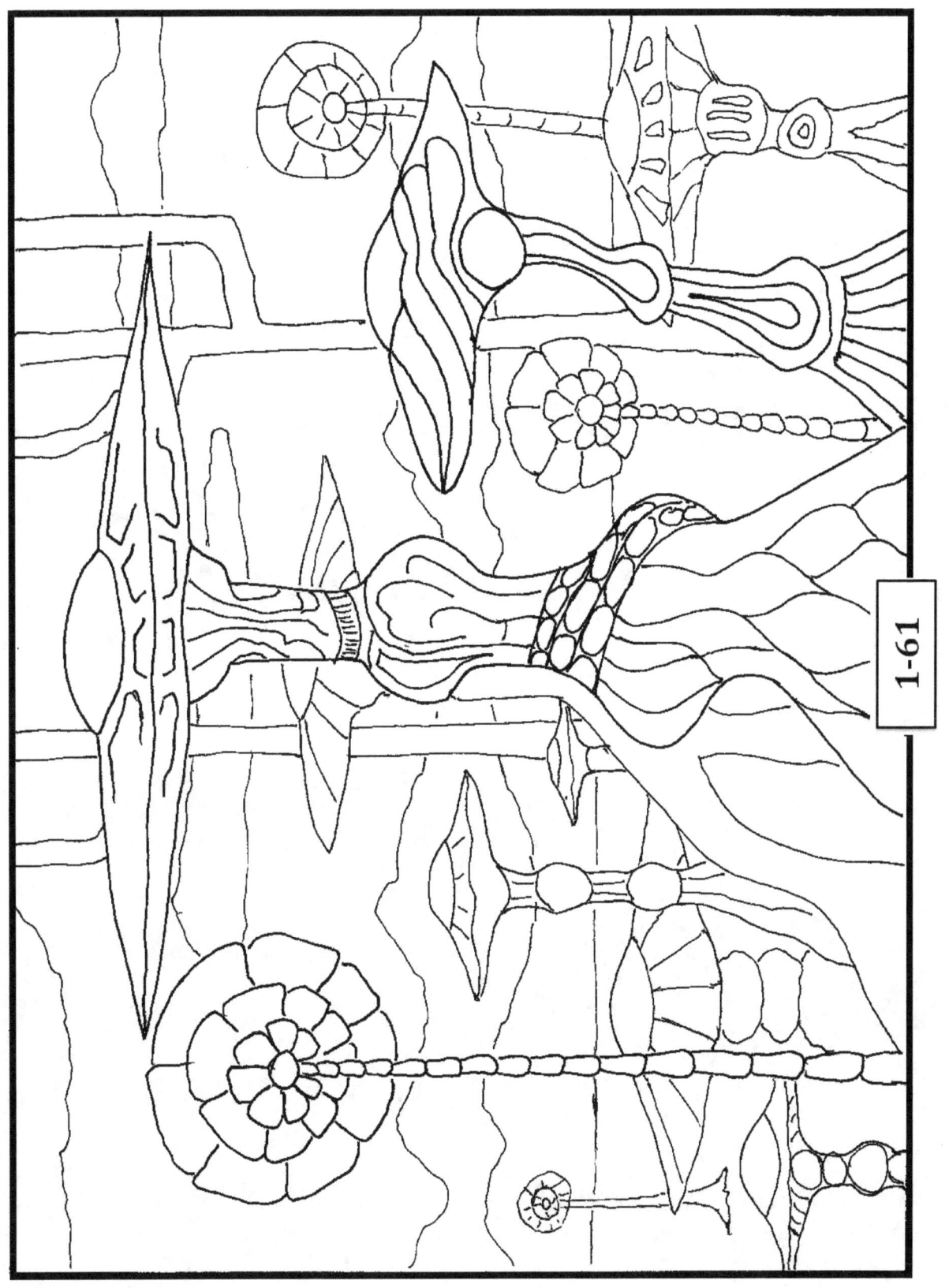

1-61

25

www.sandru.com

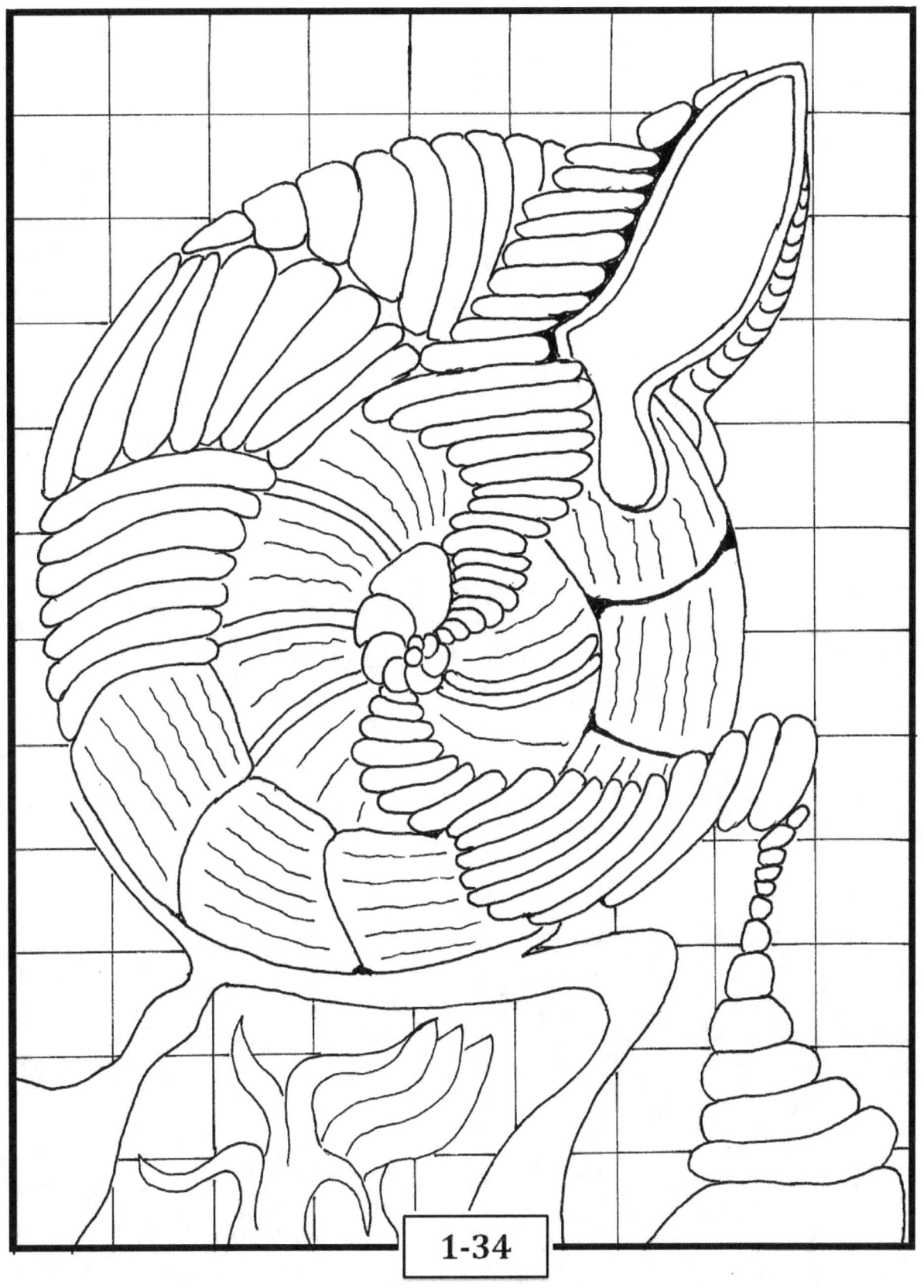

1-34

27

www.sandru.com

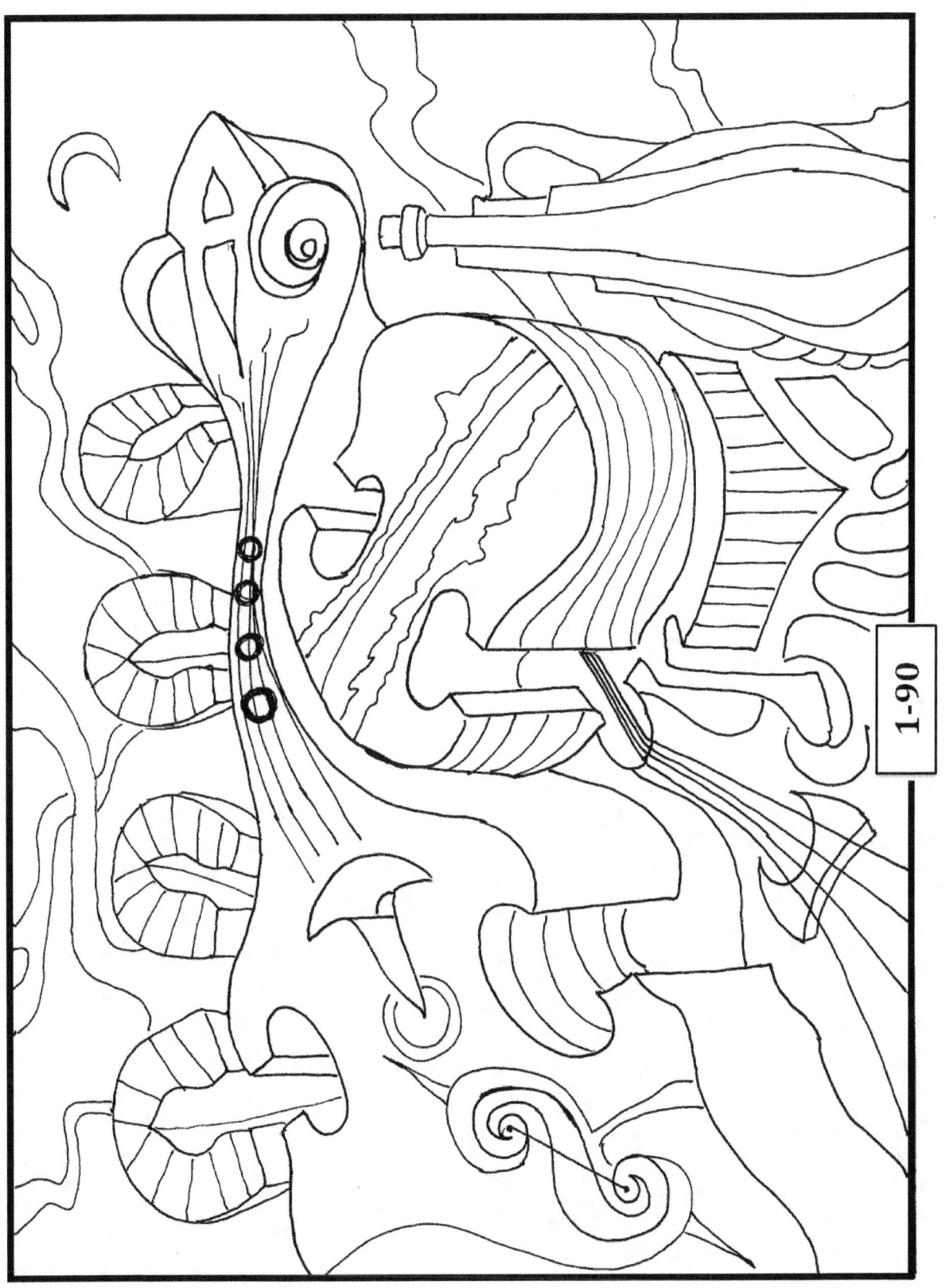

www.sandru.com

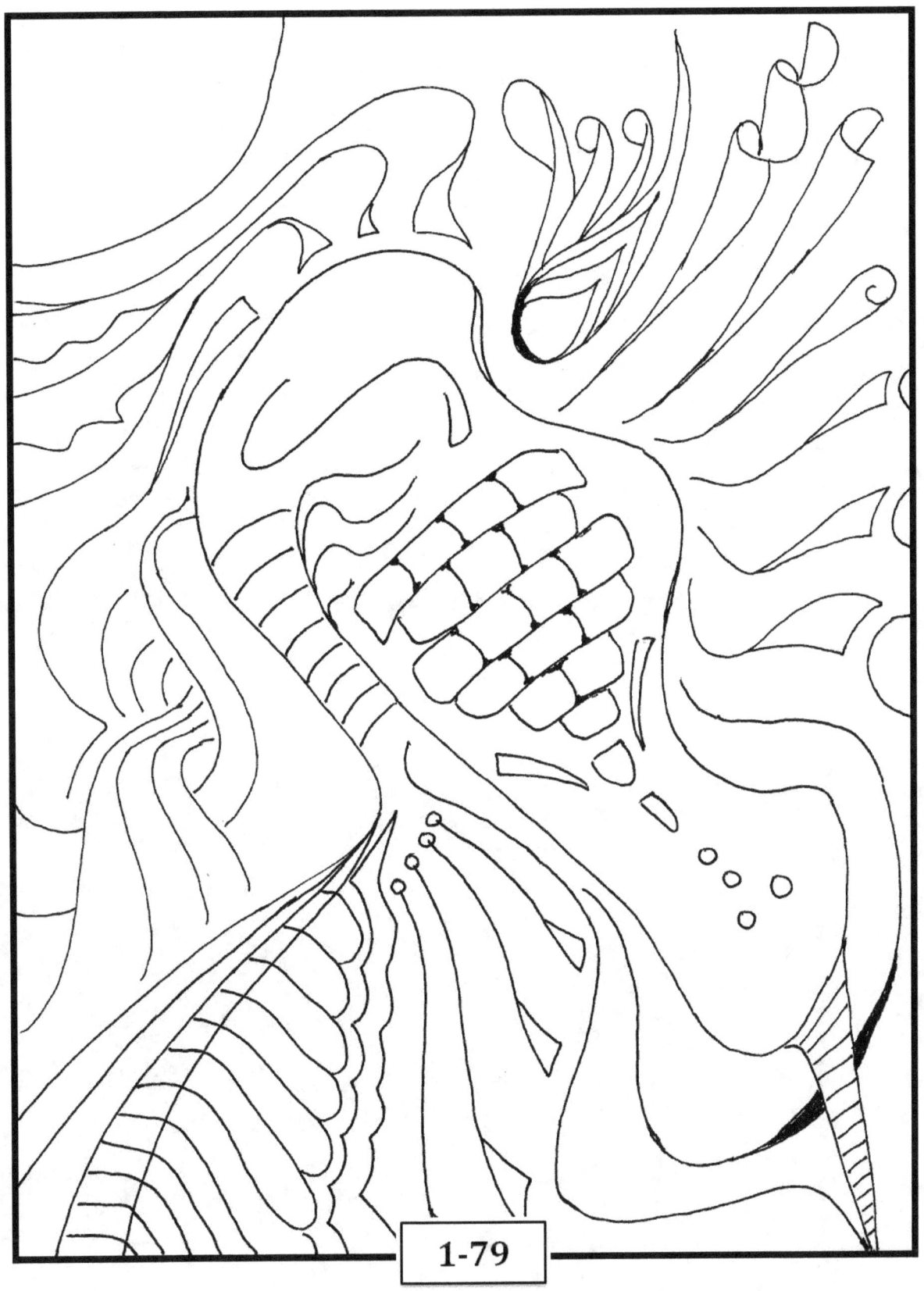

1-79

www.sandru.com

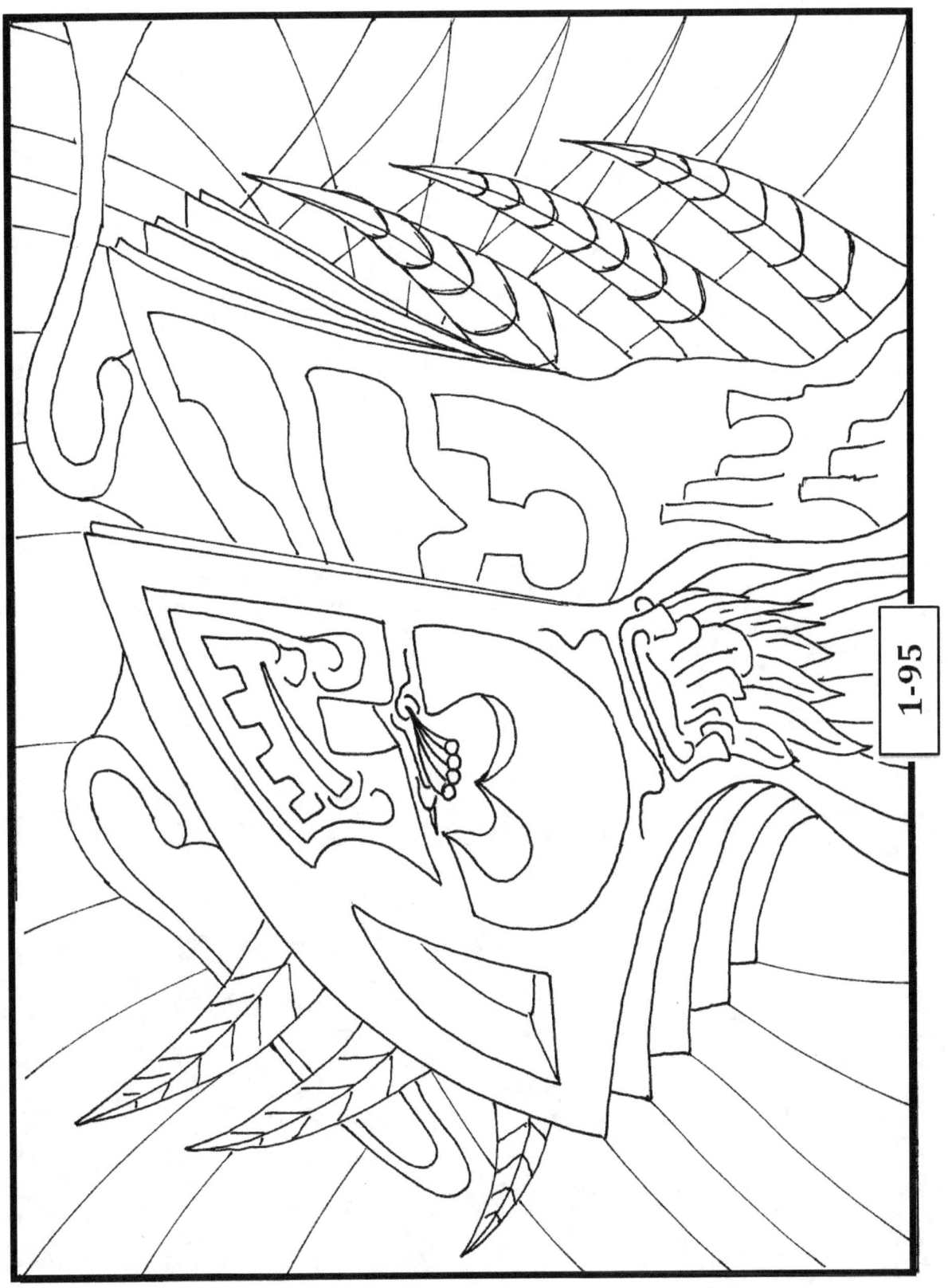

1-95

33

www.sandru.com

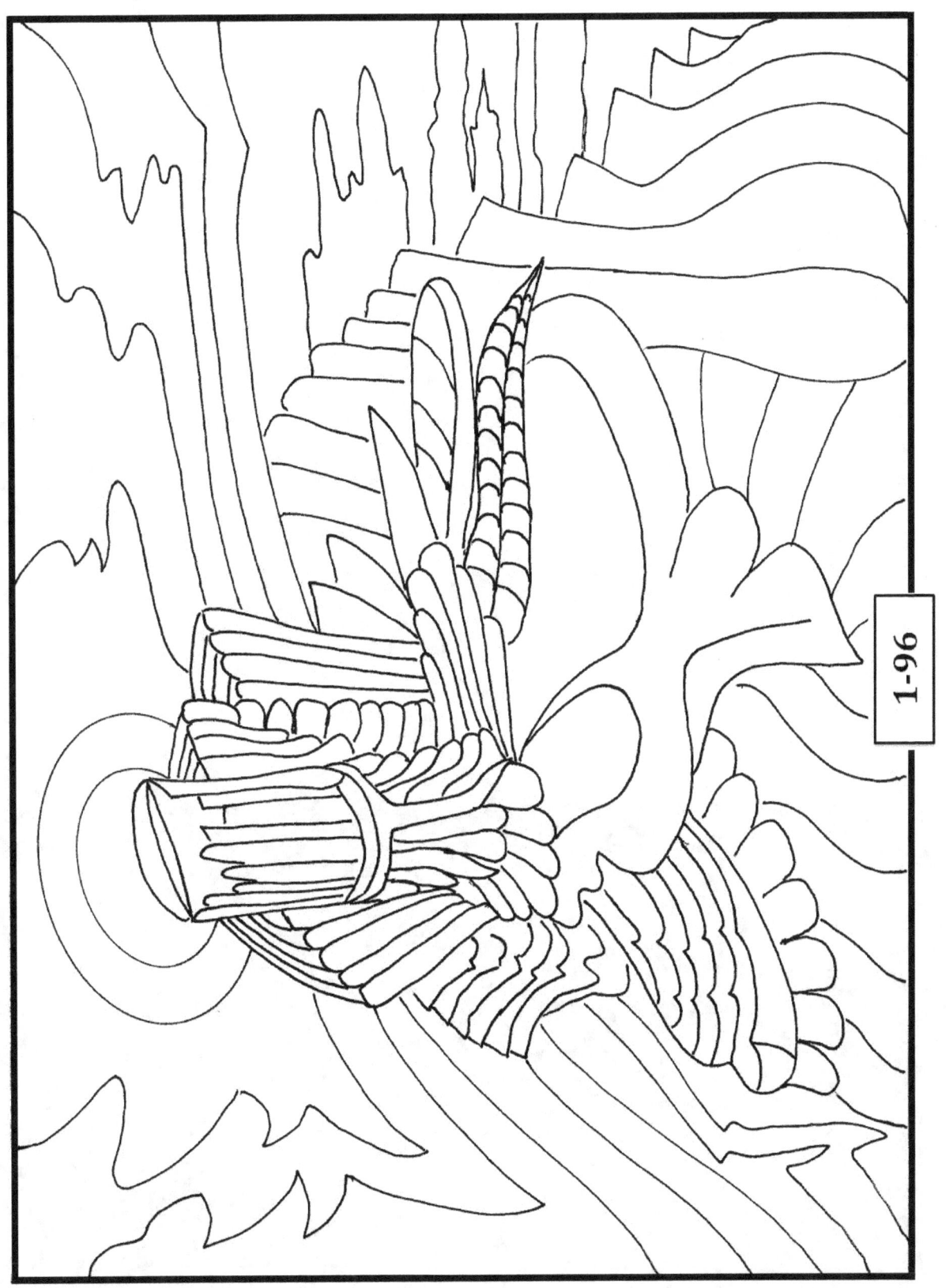

1-96

www.sandru.com

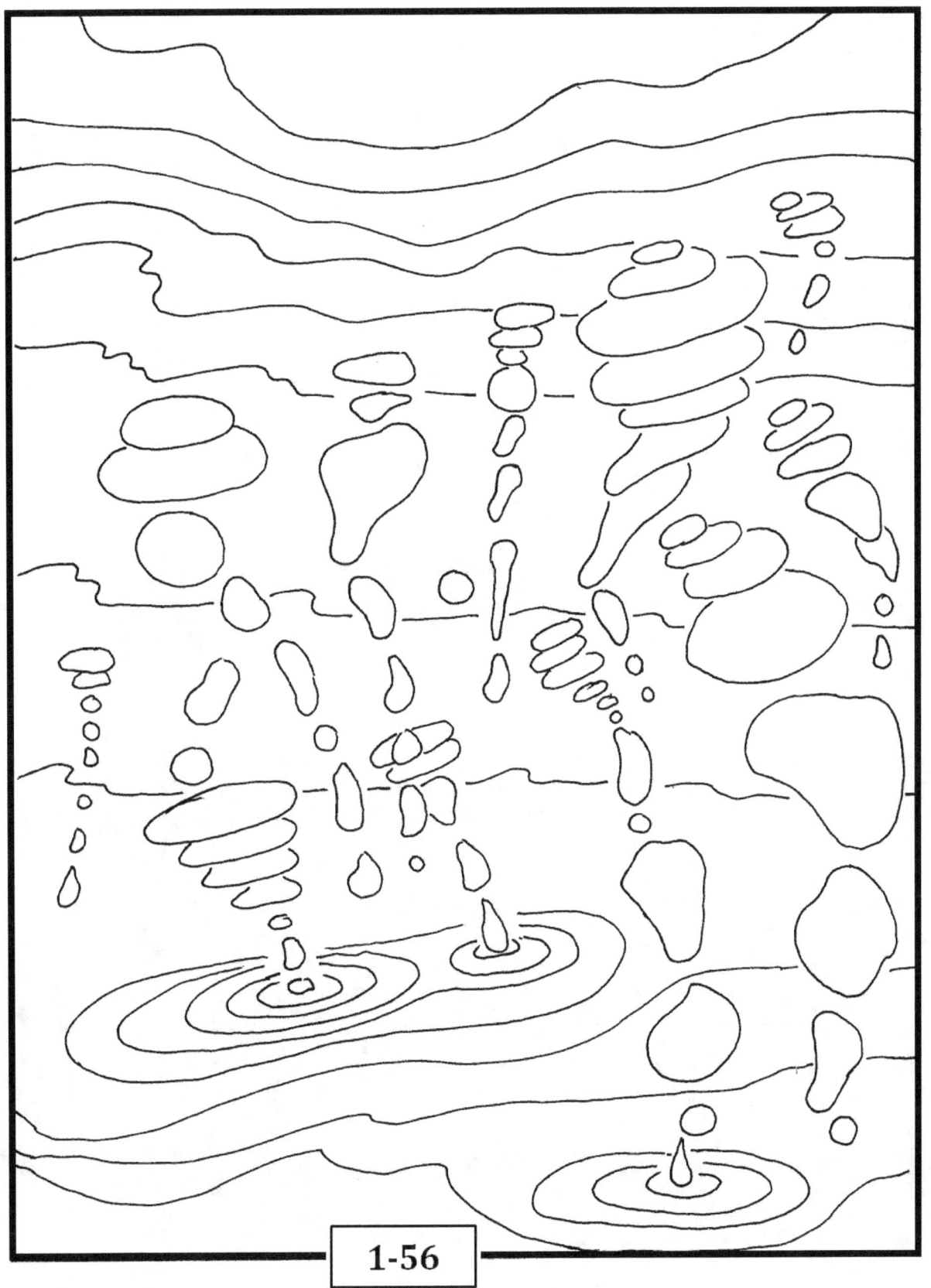

1-56

www.sandru.com

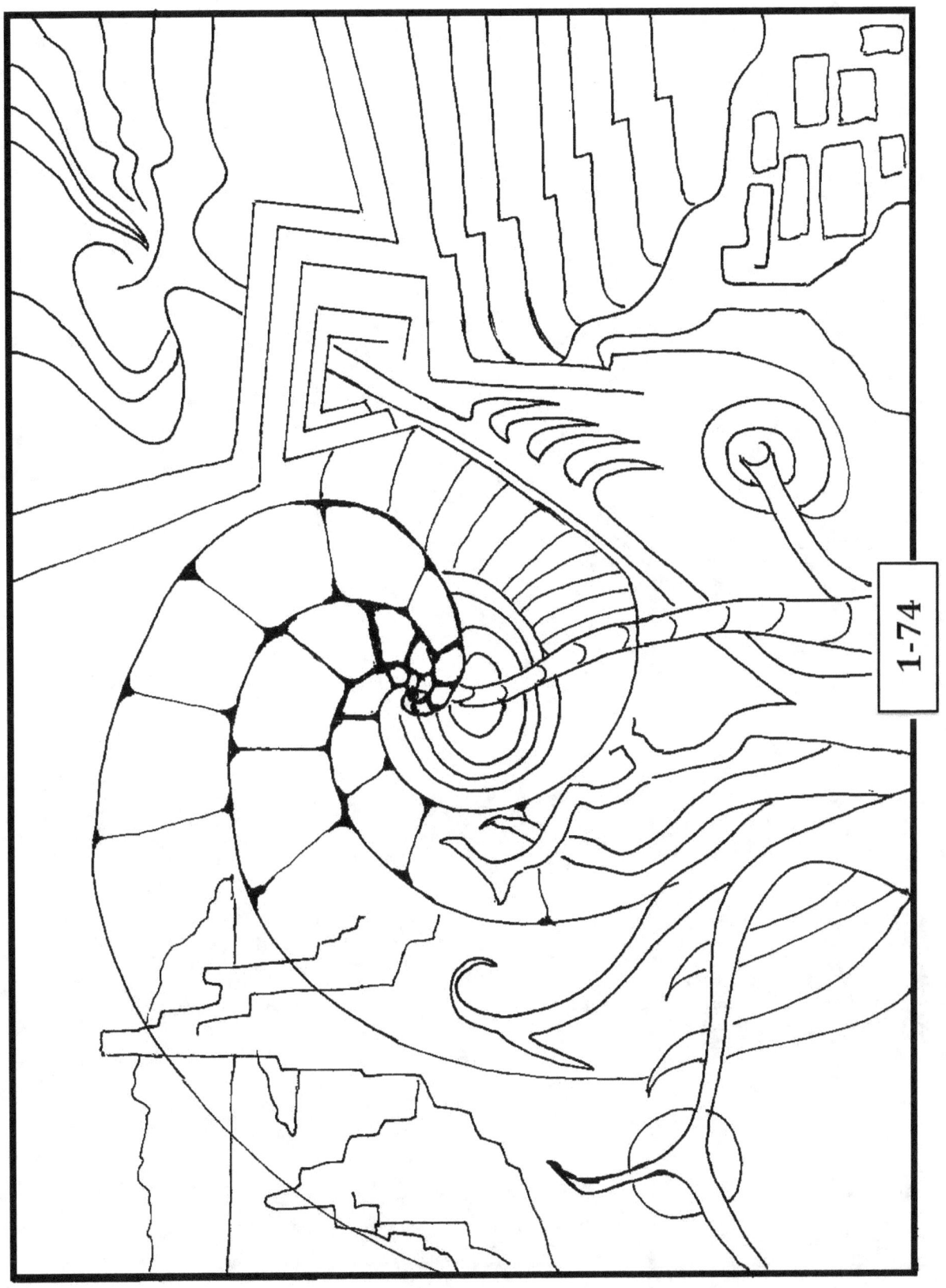

1-74

www.sandru.com

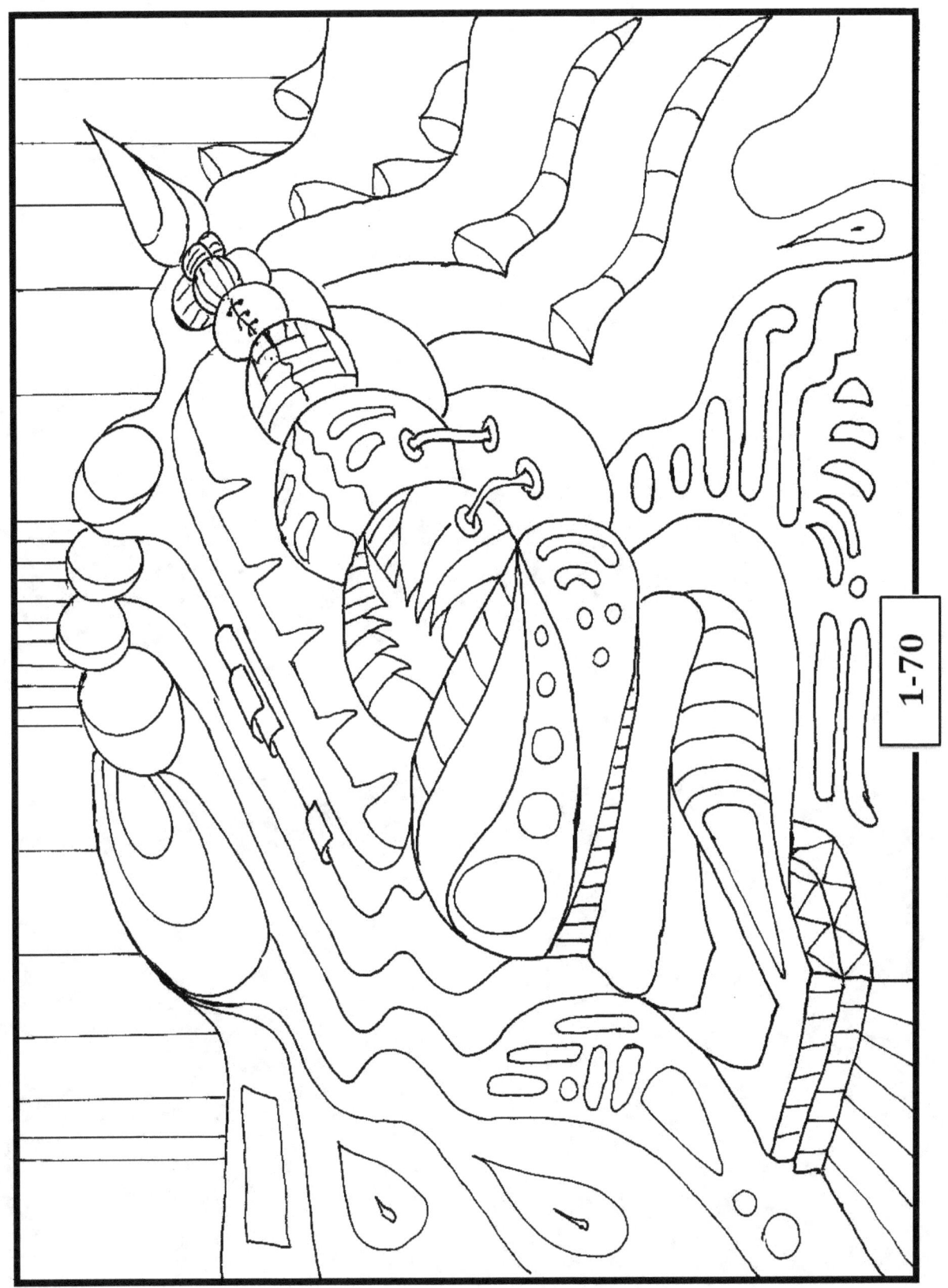

1-70

www.sandru.com

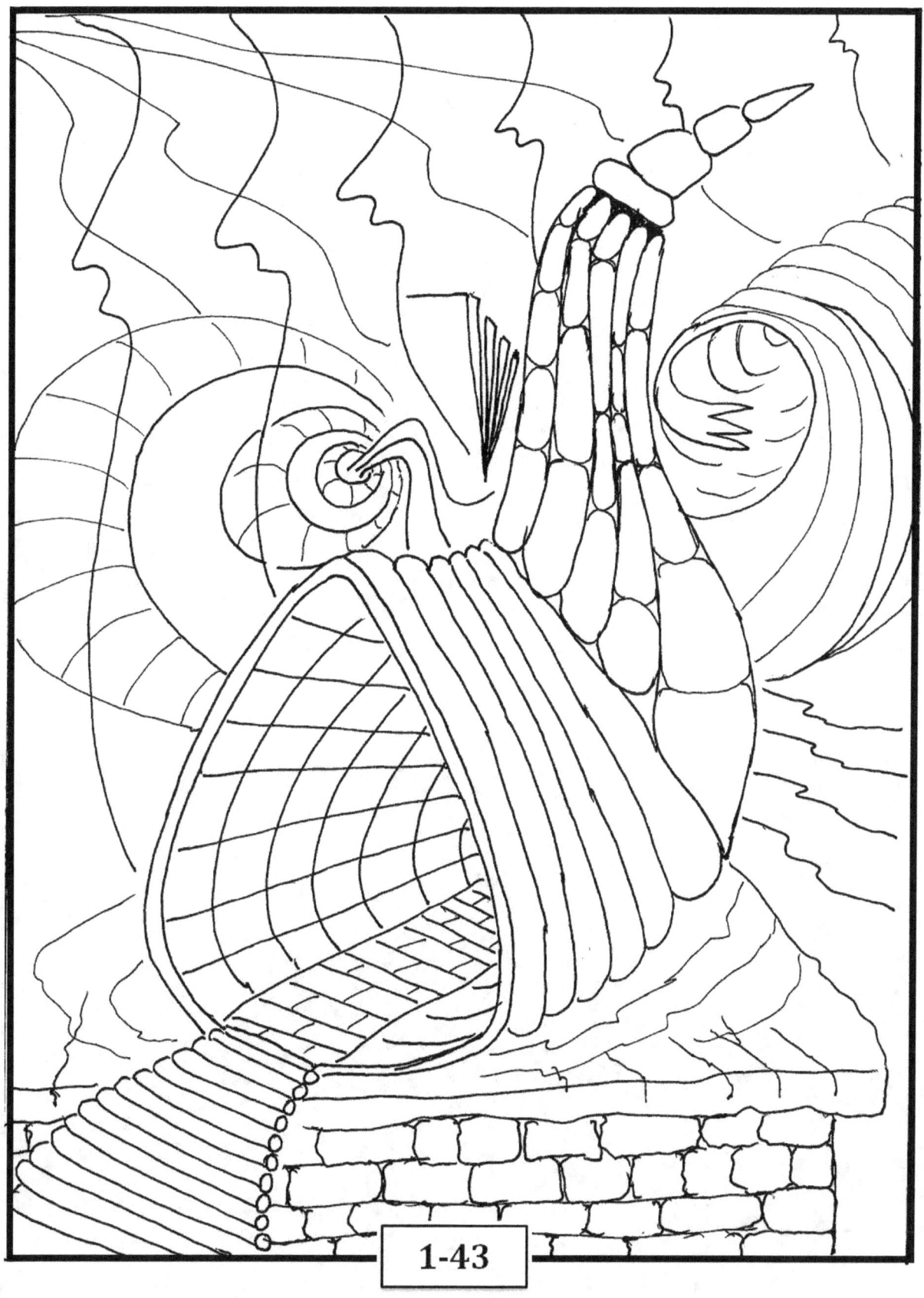

1-43

www.sandru.com

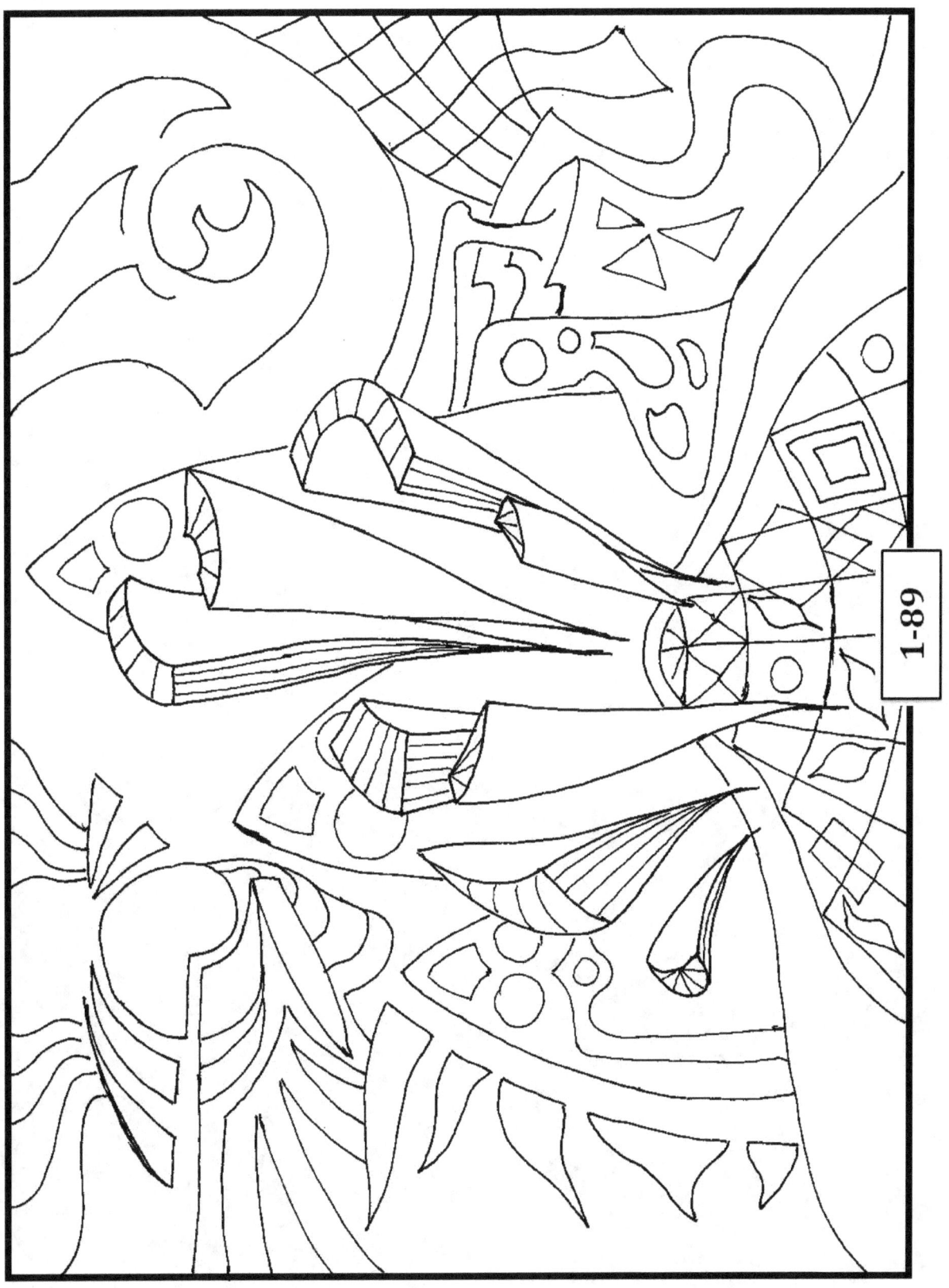

1-89

www.sandru.com

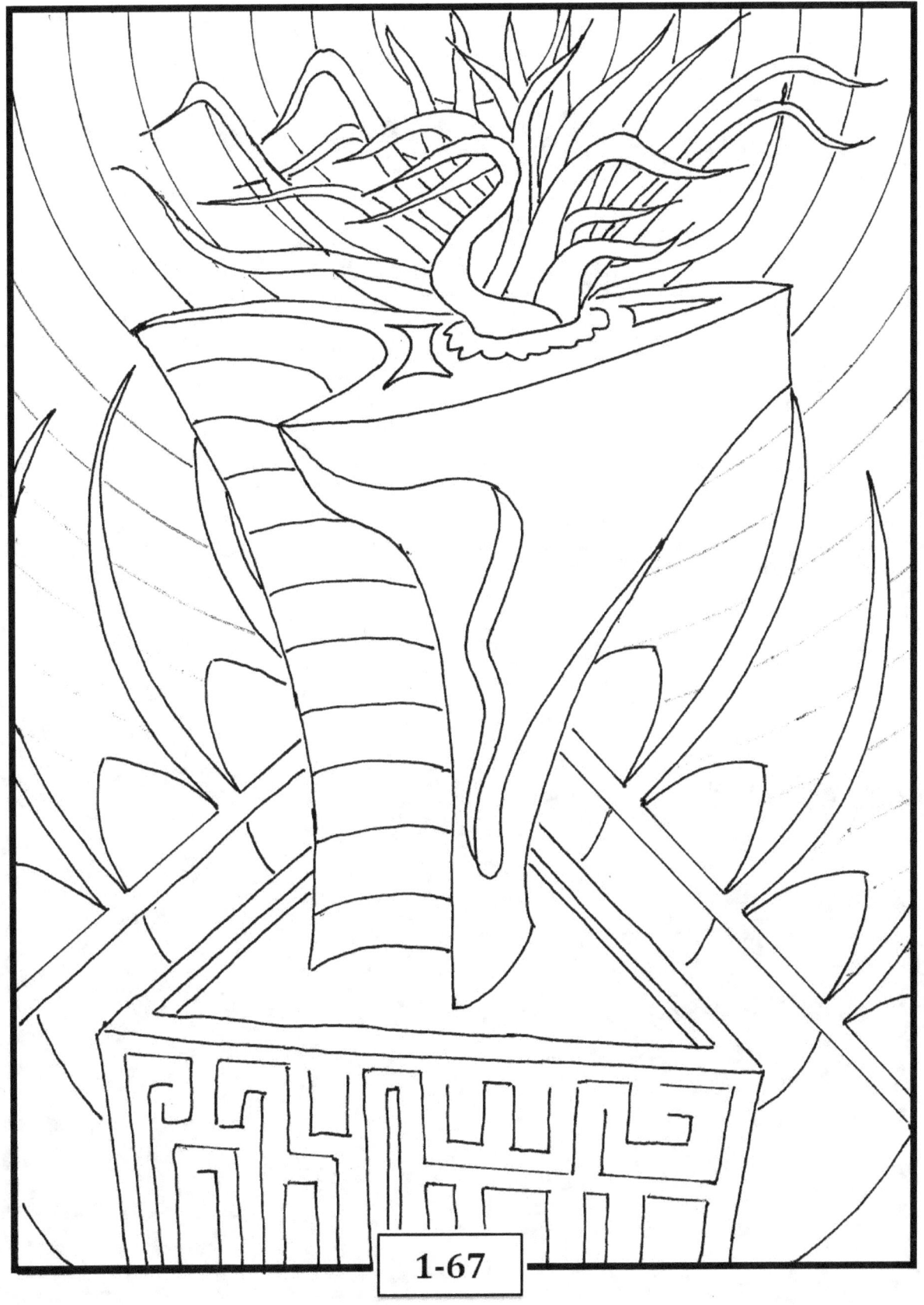

1-67

www.sandru.com

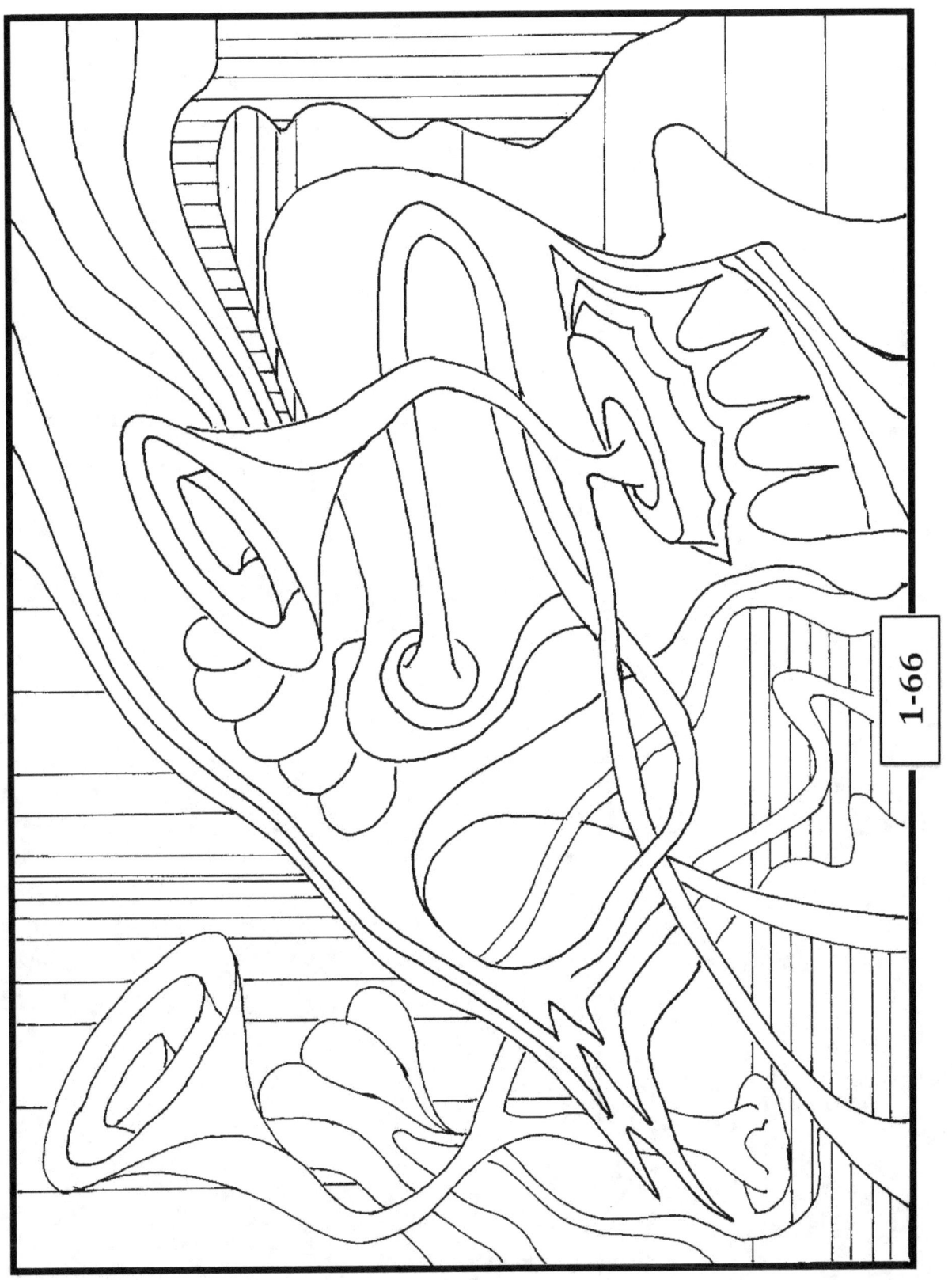

1-66

www.sandru.com

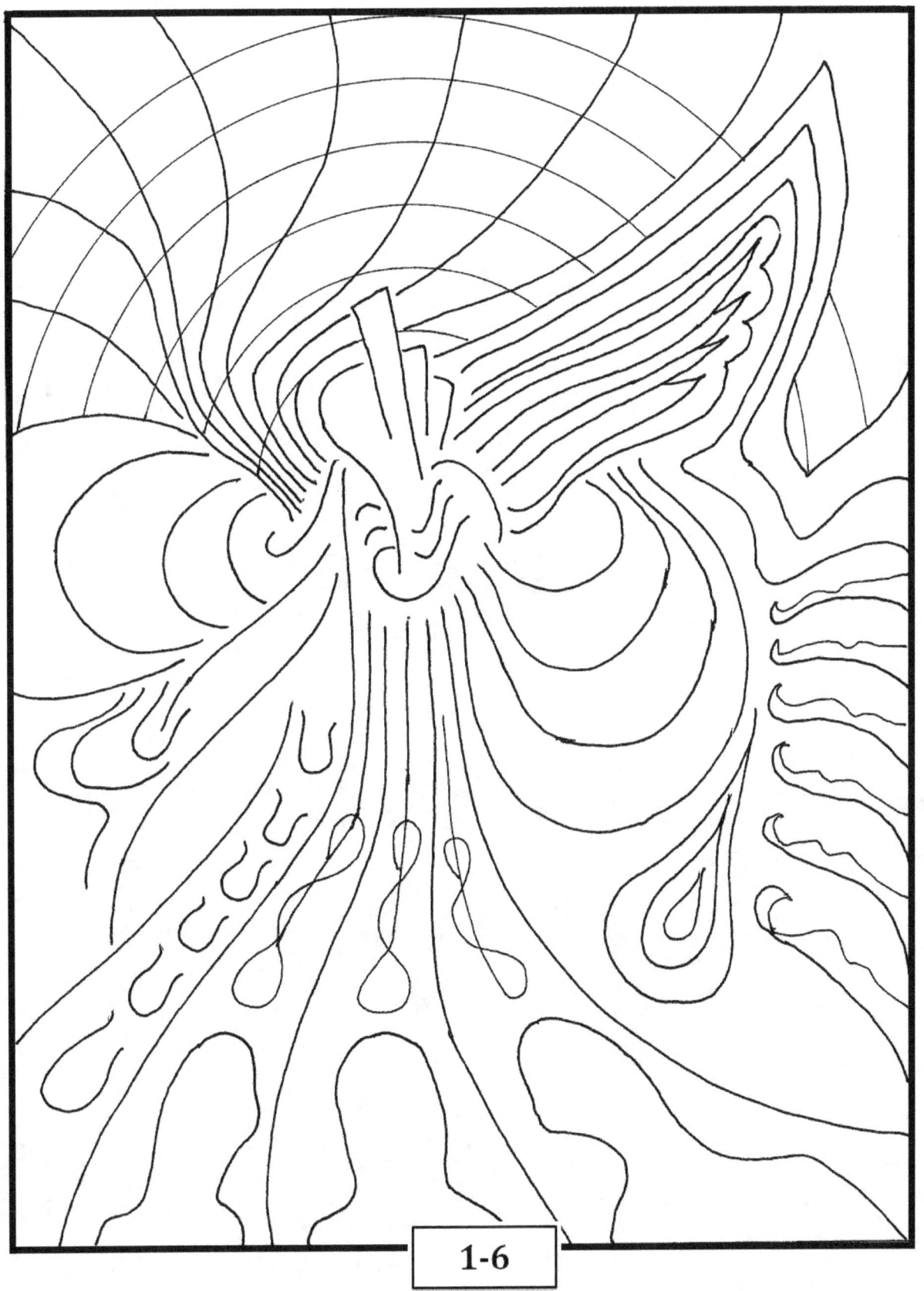

1-6

www.sandru.com

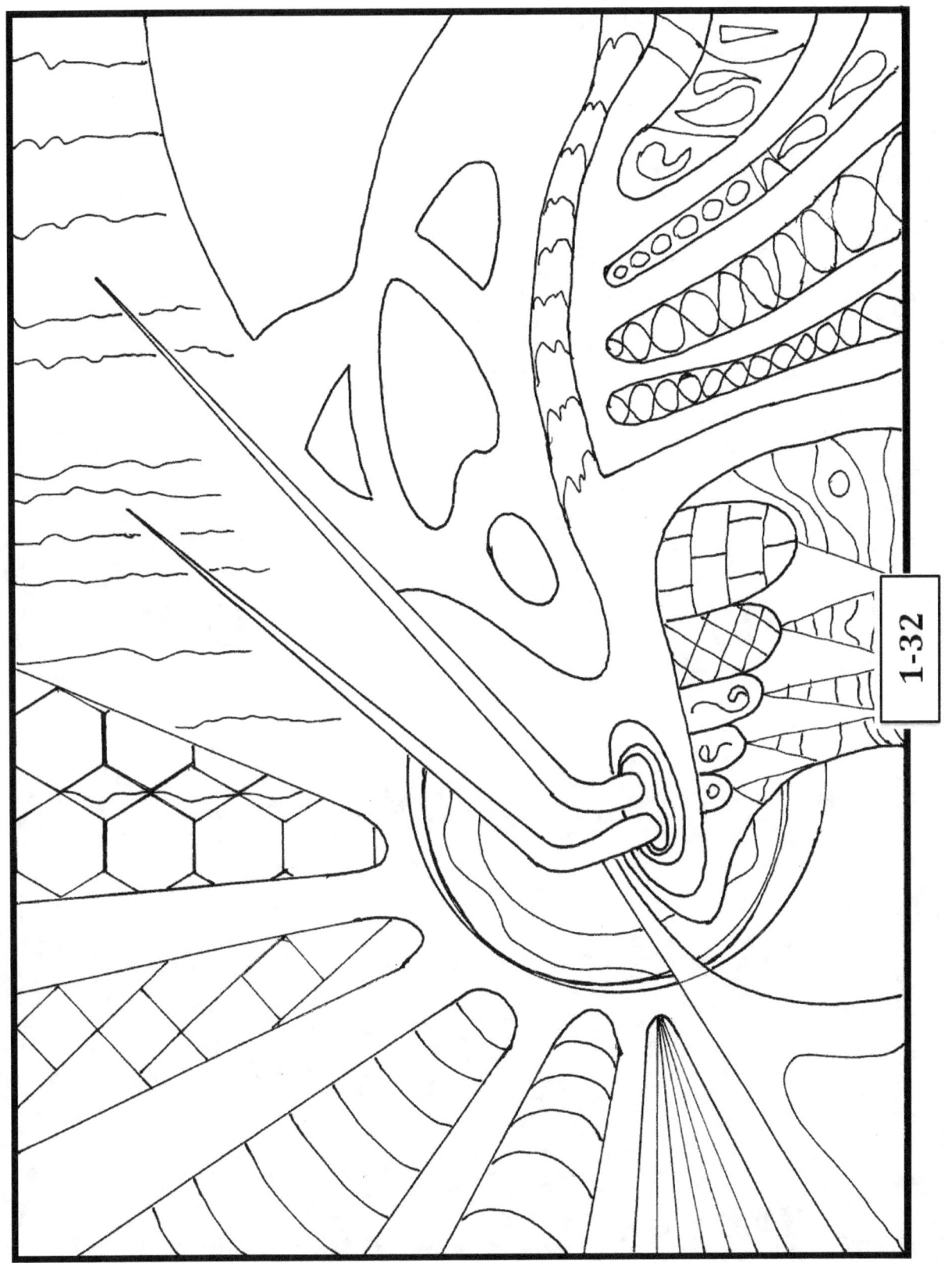

1-32

www.sandru.com

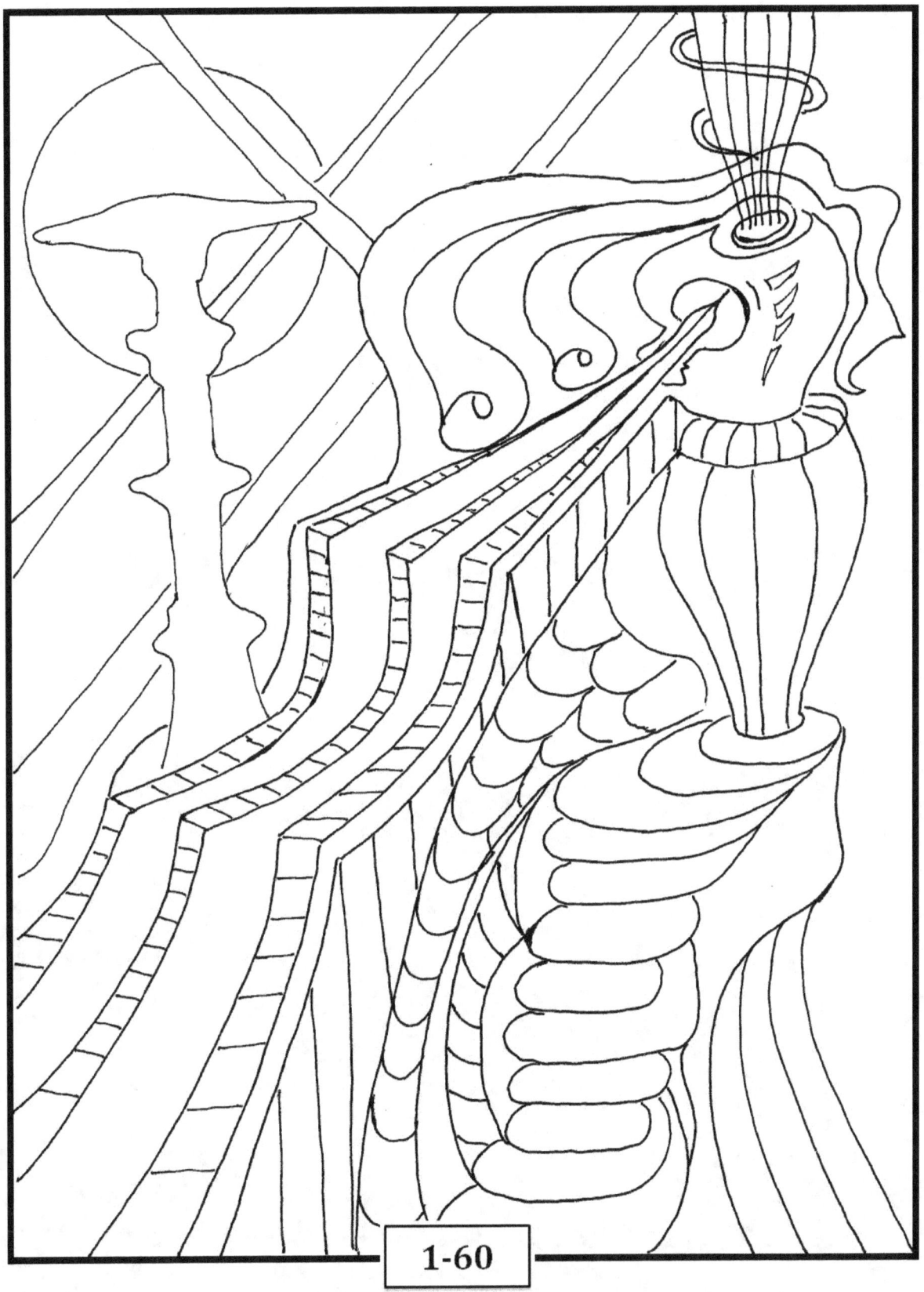

1-60

www.sandru.com

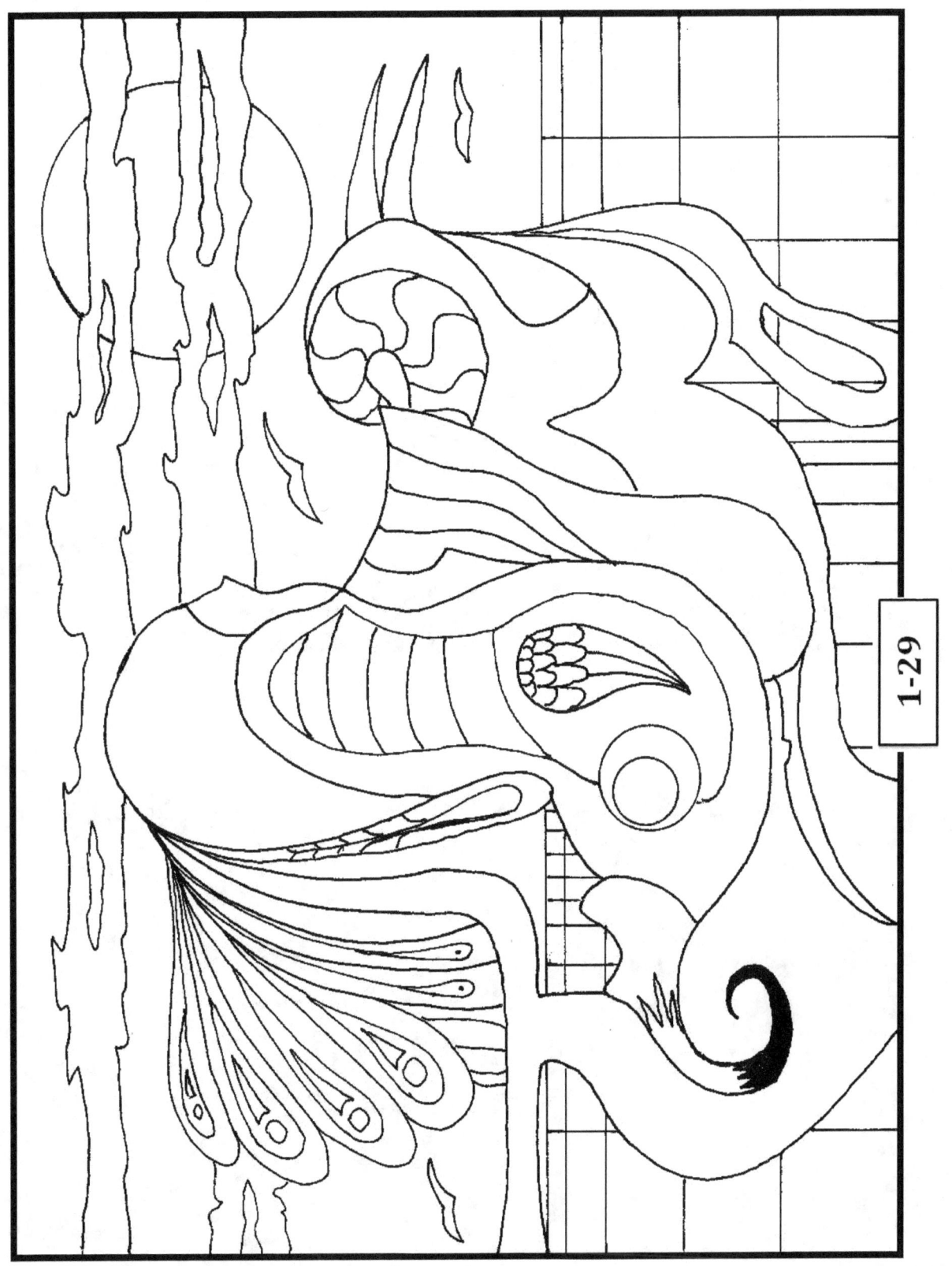

1-29

57

www.sandru.com

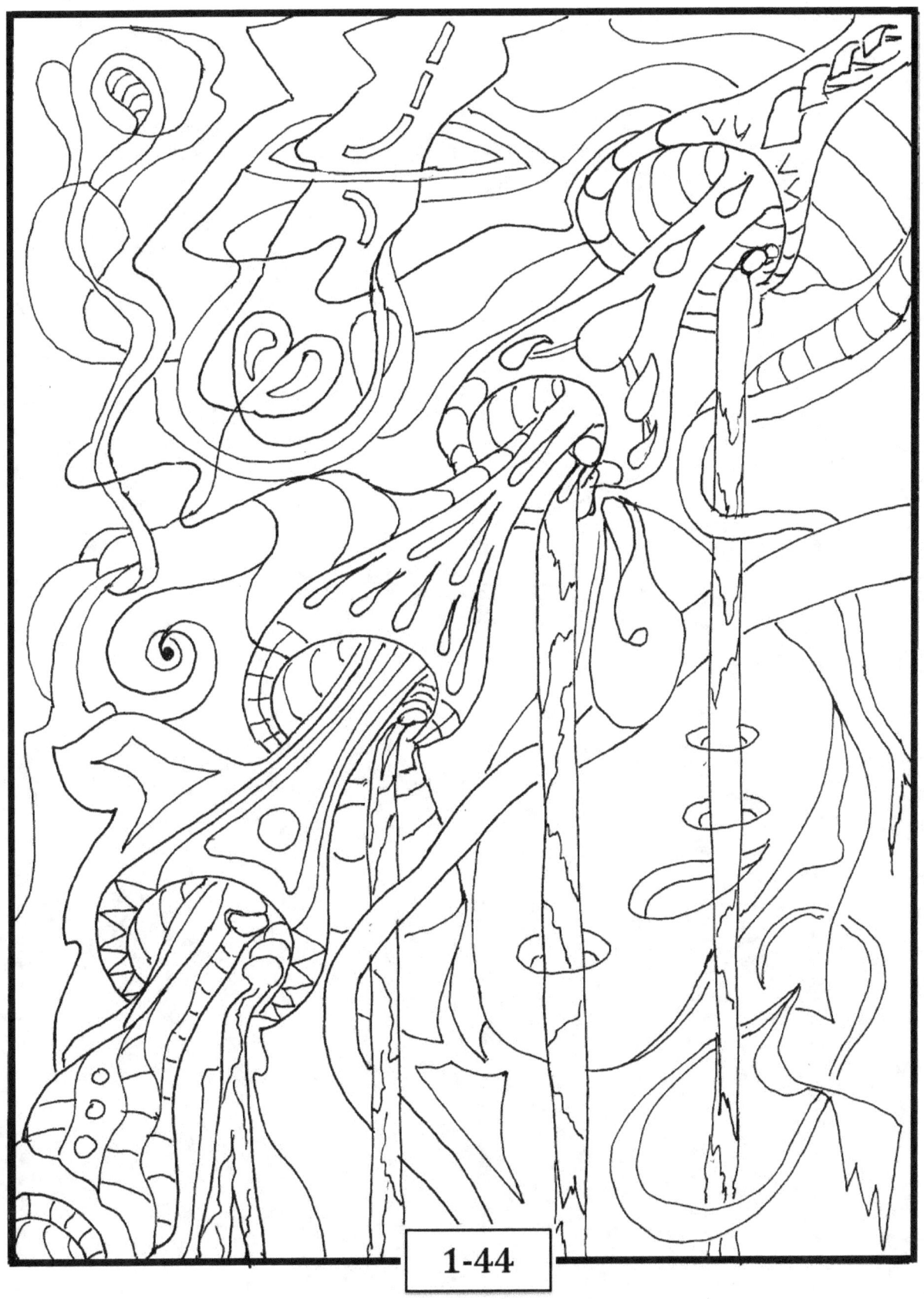

1-44

www.sandru.com

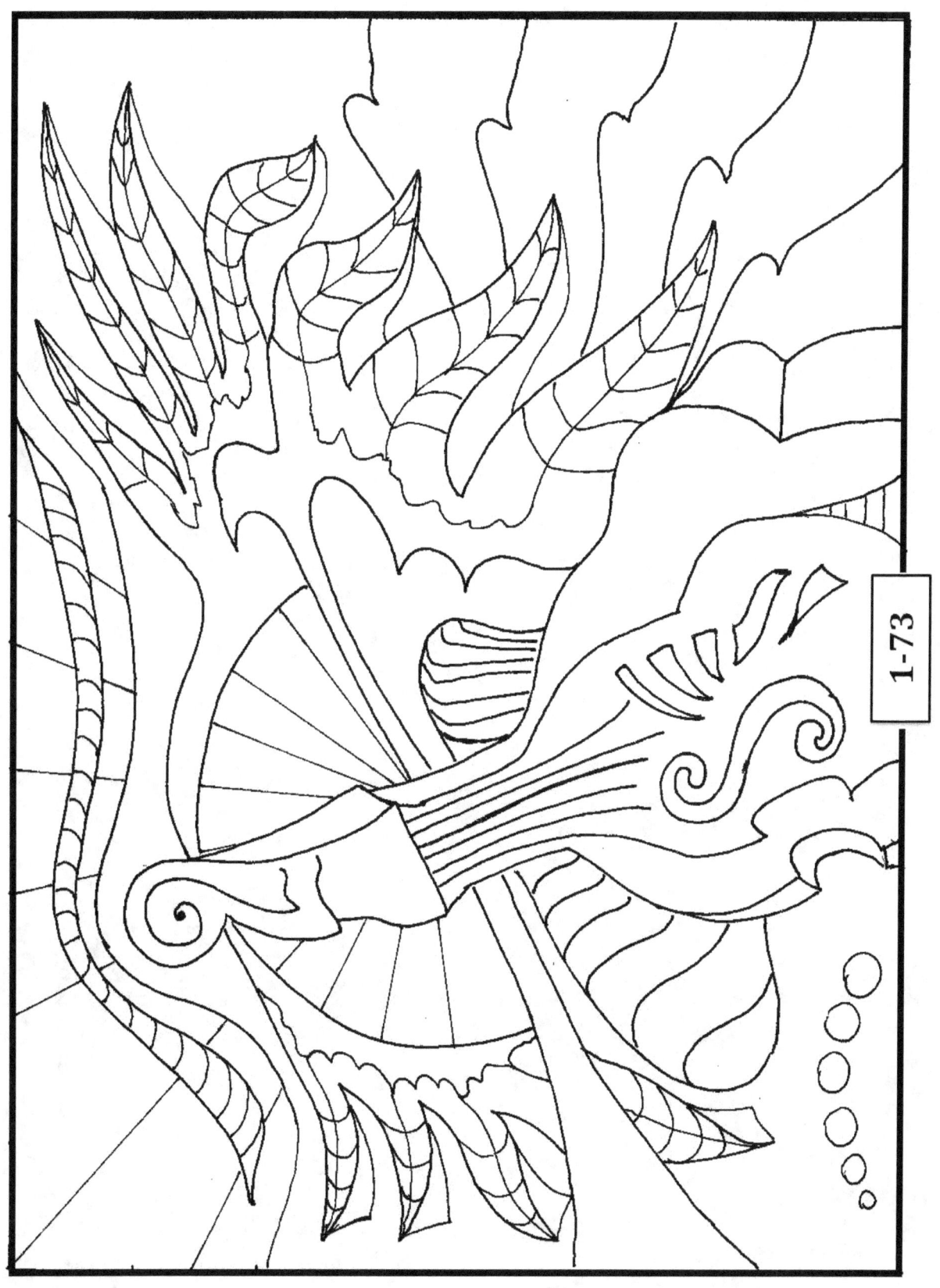

1-73

www.sandru.com

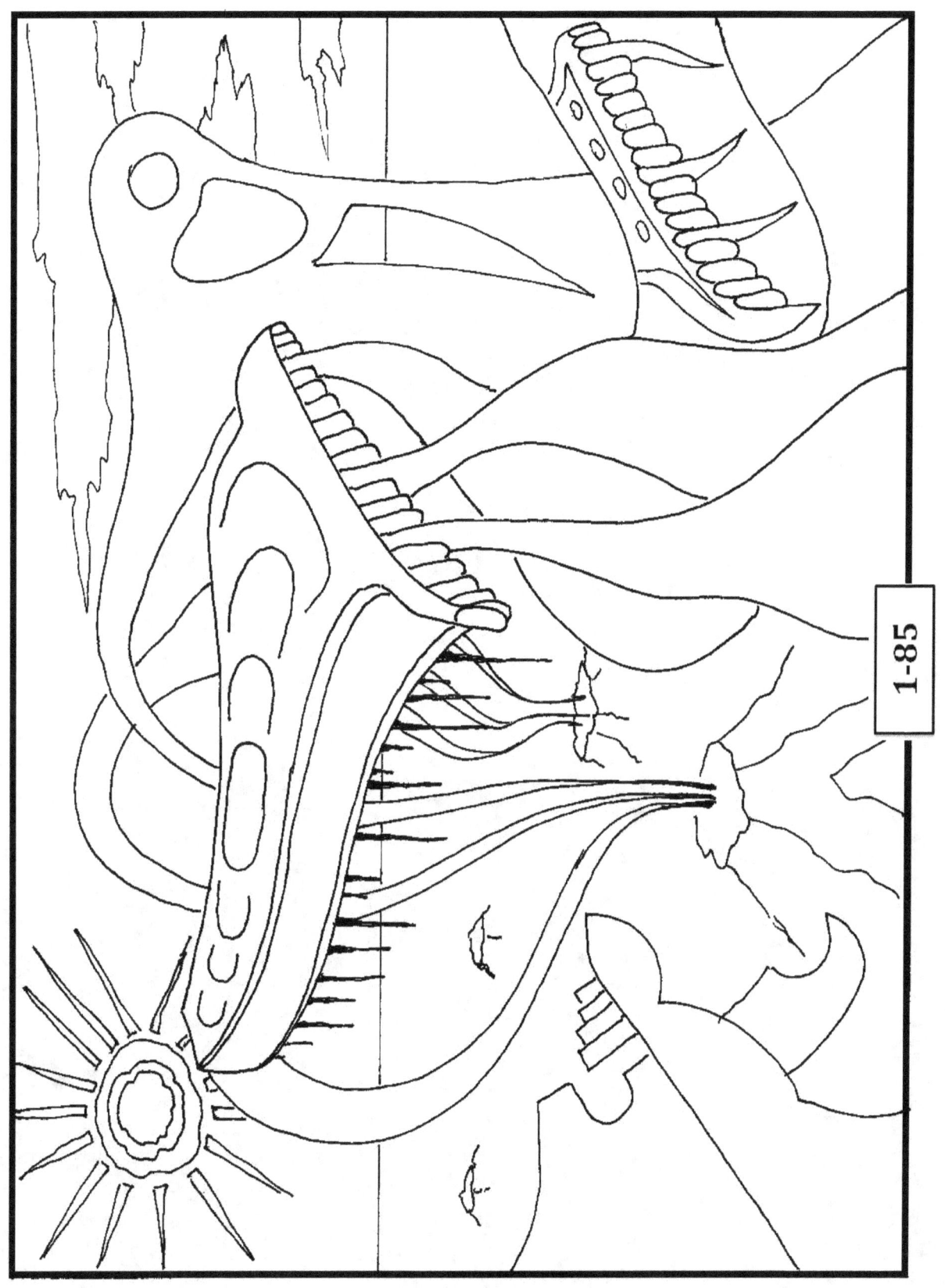

1-85

63

www.sandru.com

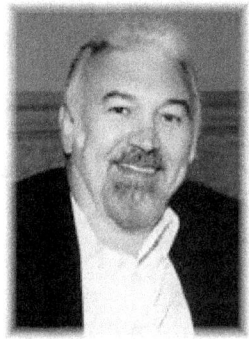About Dumitru "Mit" Sandru

He was born in the greater area of Transylvania in the last century. He is an artist, composer, and author. He paints in the classical, surreal, and modern styles, and most of the music Dumitru composes is of the New Age flavor. As an author, he prefers to write Science-Fiction, Paranormal, and Teen/Children Fantasy novels.

Dumitru resides in California with his wife. They have one daughter and two grandsons.

Books authored by the artist:
The Vlad V Series, Blue Blood Vampires Thriller & Romance:

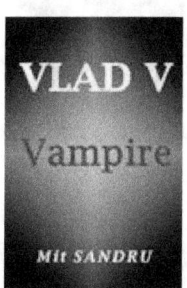

Vampire (Vlad V, Book 1) by Mit Sandru. Meeting a vampire isn't something that happens every night, even on the New York City subways. Even in her wildest dreams Cat never expected to meet a vampire or survive an encounter with one. Instead, she becomes his confidant. Why is she so lucky?

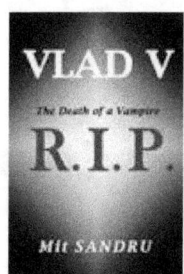

R.I.P., The Death of a Vampire (Vlad V, Book 2) by Mit Sandru. The US intelligence agencies have a massive database, including pictures that can identify any person in the US and abroad. A search has found a photograph of Vlad V Draculesti, a man living in present-day Manhattan, dating from 1851. How can that be? Why does Vlad look the same in the 21st century as he did in the 19th? Who is this man who has lived such a long life? Homeland Security Federal Agent John Miller discovers that Vlad V Draculesti is a vampire, and he blackmails Vlad for billions of dollars, threatening to divulge that information to the authorities or to the evil Dr. Hellinherr, who is trying to create a super-race of people through the use of vampire blood. But Vlad V, because of a mishap, is now dying of old age, and all he wants is to die in peace. Cat Sanders, his great-granddaughter, and his three vampire friends—François, Angelique, and Mundibuto—come to his rescue. They foil the intelligence agencies' plans to discover the real identity of Vlad V Draculesti, and they eliminate the corrupt federal agent's threat. Never underestimate a vampire, his cunning great-granddaughter and his vampire friends.

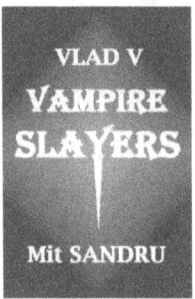

Vampire Slayers (Vlad V, Book 3) by Mit Sandru. Vlad V the vampire warned Cat that when you're rich, the stakes are much higher, and that she might have to do appalling things to survive. Cat thought she'd have to deal with unscrupulous lawyers, greedy financiers and bankers, Wall Street shysters, corrupt politicians, devious conmen, and depraved socialites. Instead, an old nemesis allied with a vampire-slayer drug cult came out of the dark, demanding extortion money or she would be killed. Capturing a vampire—Vlad V perhaps—would be an added bonus for the cult. Blue vampire blood could provide perpetual life and additional riches. Unfortunately, the villains don't know who or what they are dealing with. Never upset the great-granddaughter of Vlad V and Angelique, her vampire friend, if you want to stay healthy and alive.

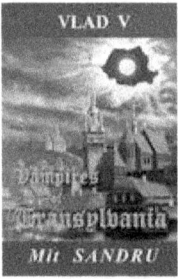

Vampires of Transylvania (Vlad V, Book 4) Cat has a simple task ahead of her: spread Vlad V Draculesti's ashes in Transylvania at midnight during a full moon. But it won't be that simple. She comes across Vlad V and Vlad the Impaler's old enemies and a sinister plot concocted by the Queen of Vampires. By discovering the queen's plot, Cat finds herself in mortal danger. Luckily, the African vampire Mundibuto and a new friend, Dr. Tudor Lupu, come to her aid. She has to use all the tricks she can muster to stay alive and take revenge on Vlad the Impaler's assassins.

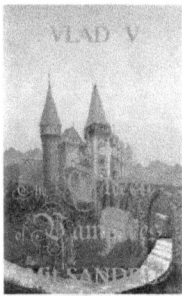

The Queen of Vampires: A New Queen Arises (Vlad V, Book 5) by Mit Sandru In Transylvania, Cat Sanders' freedom does not last long. The Vampire Queen, Eleonore von Schwarzenberg, abducts Cat and her friends after they destroyed her zombies and proto-vampires army. The Queen's revenge will be swift, painful, and deadly. Cat and her friends are in grave danger. Will they be able to avoid her wrath and survive?

Science Fiction

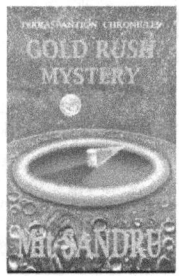

Gold Rush Mystery (Terraspantion Chronicles, Bk. 1) by Mit Sandru.   America is back on the Moon. This time, we intend to stay and establish a self-sustaining permanent base for tourism and mining. Our first lunar base is named Gold Rush. Establishing permanent life on our closest, lifeless neighbor is a challenge. But the challenge turns into a mystery when life finds us first.

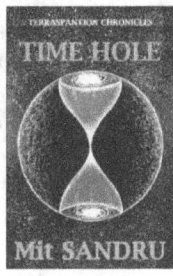

Time Hole, (Terraspantion Chronicles, Bk. 2) by Mit Sandru. Time Paradox Adventure.   The Moon has many riches, but mining them is a hazardous affair. Deedee and Arno, two lunar generalists, find perils beyond what they signed up for when traveling on the lunar surface at night . . . on the far side of the Moon. Time will not be the same after they fall into the Time Hole.

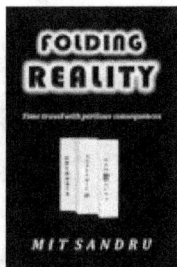

Folding Reality,   by Mit Sandru, a Paranormal, Time Travel Adventure.   Experiencing a new reality is just a paper-fold away for Mike the insurance salesman. But those realities are not by his choice and he ends up being crucified, or gassed at Auschwitz, or marooned in space in a Russian capsule.

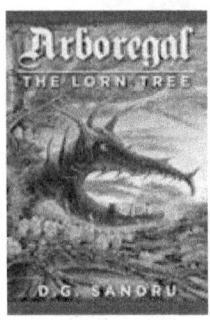

Arboregal, the Lorn Tree, by D.G. Sandru, a Teen Fantasy and Science Fiction adventure. Four young Americans are magically transported to a world where monsters roam the land, magnificent trees support all life, and an evil spirit hunts one of them to fulfill a deadly prophecy.

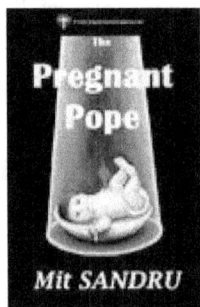

The Pregnant Pope (TIO Series), by Mit Sandru. In the year of Satan, 2066, the structure of the physical world is cracking, and inexplicable paranormal forces are interfering with humanity. The Trinity Investigation Organization, or TIO—a paranormal detective society—is the last protection against the demons, evil spirits, fanatical criminals, and sadists who are trying to destroy the world. The 92-year-old Pope is pregnant. Although he hasn't undergone any medical procedures, he carries a human fetus in his abdomen. Is this a case of self-cloning, or is it a mutation? Is this an immaculate conception, or is it Satan's work? Claire, Travis, and Prescott, the members of the Capuchin Trinity Team of TIO, are tasked with uncovering the truth about this unusual case and resolving the mystery of whether the Pope is carrying the new Messiah or the Antichrist, and who did it. Their job is to go beyond the physical world into the mind and the spiritual realm, discover a thousand-year-old connection, perform an exorcism, and fight the devil Zepar, while evading the villains who keep trying to assassinate them.

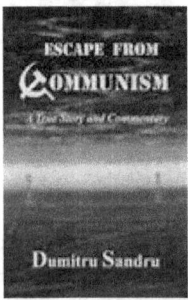

Escape from Communism, by Dumitru Sandru, a True Story and Commentary. Life under communism is cruel and inhumane. Communist countries have a "Berlin Wall" around them, and the whole country is a giant concentration camp. I risked my life to escape from hell and reach freedom.

Visit him at **www.sandru.com**

www.ingramcontent.com/pod-product-compliance
Lightning Source LLC
Chambersburg PA
CBHW081749220526
45468CB00008B/2300